TOOLS & TRADES
OF AMERICA'S PAST

The Mercer Museum Collection

by Marilyn Arbor

With Contributions by John W. Hulbert and James R. Blackaby

ILLUSTRATORS:

Jean R. Brown • Barbara Hill Shankle • Dorothy P. Young

DESIGNER:

Lawrence Gaynor

COVER DESIGN:

Rob Larsen

COVER PHOTOGRAPHY:

John Hoenstine

THE MERCER MUSEUM • BUCKS COUNTY HISTORICAL SOCIETY

84 SOUTH PINE STREET, DOYLESTOWN, PA 18901 • (215) 345-0210

Production Management:
Tower Hill Press

All graphics based on the collection of
The Mercer Museum of The Bucks County
Historical Society, Doylestown, Bucks
County, Pennsylvania

1st edition, 1981

2nd edition, 1994

ISBN 0-910302-12-X
Library of Congress Catalog
Card No. 94-077922
Printed in the United States of America

Table of Contents

Foreword

Henry C. Mercer (1856-1930)

Owned and operated by The Bucks County Historical Society, the Mercer Museum is the outgrowth of one man's intense interest in, and enthusiasm for, the material culture of America. In 1880 Henry Chapman Mercer was a founding member of the Bucks County Historical Society, and by 1900 he was actively collecting objects which would "illustrate the daily life of a people at a given time." In 1913 Mercer offered to donate his collection of some 15,000 objects to the Society and to build a concrete, fireproof building to hold the collections.

The multi-storied, castle-like "New Museum" opened to the public in 1916 with Henry Mercer as curator. Until his death in 1930, he attempted to classify, explain, and add to the museum's collection of material culture. Pamphlets on food, clothing, and tools were published to describe certain exhibits in the museum, and plaster of Paris labels were made up to identify the exhibit rooms and specific objects.

After 1930 many more objects were added to the collection, and exhibit rooms became piled with artifacts. These rooms and the materials in them made little sense to a lay public. The most consistent complaint about the museum was that it lacked written information. In 1977 a method for labeling each exhibit room and free standing artifacts was devised, and in 1978 a proposal was submitted to the National Endowment for the Humanities seeking funds to proceed with this labeling project. The end product of the project was to be a book which would combine all of the label information into one informative package. NEH was receptive to the proposal and funded the project.

In addition to the National Endowment's support, foundation and individual support helped underwrite the cost of the book. *Tools and Trades of America's Past* functions as both a guide to the Mercer Museum collections and as a general source of information on tools and the people who used them. (Excerpted from the first edition)

For this second edition of *Tools and Trades* sections have been added and others reorganized for clarity. Added are sections on Architectural Hardware, Healing Arts, Hornsmithing and Shell Working. The section on Lighting Devices has been rewritten. This material reflects work that continued throughout the 1980's to provide written information to visitors about the museum collection. In 1989 a Changing Exhibit Gallery was established at the Mercer Museum which allows for more interpretive and thematic exhibits dealing with the collection along with Bucks County history topics. A new introduction for the second edition of Tools and Trades was written by Cory Amsler, Curator of Collections.

Douglas C. Dolan
Executive Director
The Bucks County Historical Society

"From a New Point of View": An Introduction to the 1994 Edition

It was probably one day in…1897 that I went to the premises of one of our fellow citizens, who had been in the habit of going to country sales and buying what they called 'penny lots' …When I [saw the] disordered pile of old wagons, gum-tree salt boxes, flax brakes, straw beehives, tin dinner-horns, rope machines and spinning wheels, things I had heard of but never collectively saw before, the idea occurred to me that the history of Pennsylvania was here profusely illustrated, and from a new point of view.

Henry Chapman Mercer, *1907*

This sudden and fortuitous insight led Henry Mercer on a remarkable expedition that would consume the remaining thirty-three years of his life. His goal became nothing less than the creation of a vast, comprehensive inventory of the tools and implements used by Americans before the industrial age. Mercer zealously sought to rescue and preserve the material record of the transformation from handcraft to machine production, before the artifacts vanished forever in a wave of obsolescence.

At first calling his collection, "The Tools of the Nationmaker," Mercer later came to view the title as too limiting. He observed that many of the objects used by Anglo-Saxon pioneers to "carve out an American nation" were little changed from more ancient implements then being recovered from the ruins of Greece, Rome, Egypt and the Middle East. Mercer also recognized that other global cultures had used—and in some cases were still using— similar implements to erect shelters, produce clothing and prepare food. Humans were tool makers and tool users, he realized, and American experiences could be linked with those of other cultures around the world. His collection, then, came to represent not just an epoch in American history, but the timeless striving of human beings to meet their wants and needs through the manufacture of things.

Despite Mercer's global, anthropological vision, the reality of finite resources required that he limit the collection chiefly to the artifacts of pre-industrial America, especially those made and used by European-Americans in the 17th, 18th and early-19th centuries.

In attempting to craft a new type of history in which the lives of "ordinary" people took center stage, Mercer further stressed the collection and study of common, everyday objects. It was the sickles, hammers, spinning wheels, pie plates and other examples of vernacular material culture that interested him, not the fine tea-tables, silver candlesticks or porcelain teapots which had come to be coveted by antiquarian connoisseurs.

Although he was preoccupied with collecting "tools," it must be recognized that Mercer's definition extended far beyond our common understanding of the term. Since he was interested not only in documenting changing technologies, but changing modes of life, his collecting extended to stoves, chairs, pottery, and textiles: "all things illustrating the life of a people at a given time," as he put it. As a result, the Mercer Museum collection contains the products of tinsmithing as well as the tools, the shoes made by the cordwainer as well as the implements he used to produce them. In fact, what Mercer referred to as "tools" we might today call "material culture:" objects made to meet a variety of human wants and needs.

Mercer's motivations, and his interpretation of the collection that he created, were soundly rooted in the needs and interests of his generation. Deep anxieties spawned by America's transition from a pre-industrial to an industrial and commercial society, and from a producer to a consumer culture, plagued many Americans at the turn of the 20th century. In the tools, products and lifeways of the pre-industrial craftsman, Mercer's generation sought rejuvenation. In them, they found a renewal of art, honest labor, and spiritual vitality. At the same time, the artifacts of pre-industrial life illustrated how far modern Americans had advanced, both technologically and materially, thus providing "object lessons" that both sanctioned progress and renewed confidence in the future.

But of course Mercer's collecting and scholarship reflect far more than simple nostalgia, or the search for an antidote to a changing world. Mercer pursued his work with a scientific detachment as he sought to understand and explain the patterns of human history. He seized on the artifact as the most revealing and democratic piece of evidence in historical inquiry, a choice that is not surprising considering the material abundance of the late 19th century, and the faith Victorians placed in the ability of the object to communicate ideas and values. And, he sought to make connections between past and present, thus rising above mere antiquarianism. In keeping with

the philosophy of his contemporaries in the fields of history, anthropology and folklore, Mercer believed that by scientifically charting the course of the past, one might also illuminate the course of humanity.

Today, we must seek our own meanings in the artifacts Mercer assembled. After all, our age has its own questions, concerns—and historical needs. As anxieties produced by profound social change preoccupied Mercer's generation, so too do similar concerns nag at our own conscience. Increasingly, history museums are being called upon to shed light on contemporary issues such as substance abuse, violence, environmental decay, and tolerance of gender, racial and ethnic diversity. To use artifacts in this way requires viewing them from a fresh perspective ("a new point of view" in Mercer's words). Thus, a whiskey still begins to reveal something about the persistence of alcohol abuse in America, a gallows provokes thought about capital punishment, and a wooden plane, once used by an African-American craftsman, documents the cultural diversity that has always been present in American life.

Looking at the Mercer Museum collection, or any collection, from this contemporary perspective has validity. After all, it was Mercer himself who urged us to "look from the present backward to the past." But regardless of the purposes to which we may put history or historical artifacts today, the fundamental starting point for making use of material culture continues to be an understanding of the nature and function of the objects themselves. By preserving and documenting the uses of tools and other artifacts Mercer, and others of his generation, helped lay the foundation for all subsequent attempts to derive meaning from things. This book provides a similar foundation. It, like the Mercer Museum, offers a comprehensive visual guide to the objects of early America, their uses and physical contexts. If every person can indeed be his or her own historian, connecting the present to a usable past, perhaps you can derive new meaning, new importance, from the tools and artifacts that Henry Mercer began assembling nearly one hundred years ago.

Cory M. Amsler
Curator of Collections
Mercer Museum/
Bucks County Historical Society

Architectural Hardware

1700-1860
Hardware Styles:
Three Periods

The hardware used in American homes changed both in style and form during the 18th and 19th centuries. Important at first as a highly-visible decorative element, hardware gradually became a less noticed, though better-functioning utilitarian object. Changing consumer tastes, the development of new materials and technologies, the transition from handcraft to factory production, and the need for hardware in greater quantity all contributed to the changing appearance of hardware.

Acceptance of new styles, improvements and innovations in architectural hardware occurred slowly and unevenly. In rural areas and small communities, lack of access to new hardware products and the conservative tastes of residents sometimes perpetuated earlier forms and styles of hardware.

The blacksmith or locksmith who made hardware was an important source of continuity. To his craft he brought centuries of accumulated skill and experience, influenced by the tradition of craftsmanship common to his homeland. Even as hardware changed, traditional smiths in some areas continued to fashion hand-wrought latches, hinges and locks for their customers.

Traditional Hardware

Since medieval times, craftsmen had designed hardware to attract attention. They worked by hand, competing with each other to produce distinctive or intricate designs. They made decorative latches and hinges to embellish otherwise rough or plain woodwork. Their large and impressive locks symbolized security and social position. Such visible ironwork attested to the skill of the craftsman, advertised the status of the homeowner or emphasized the importance of a building.

Primitive woodworking technology also contributed to the appearance of hardware. A crude batten-type door or shutter needed long strap hinges to keep it square. Setting a lock into a door required difficult and expensive labor. So, house builders mounted locks on door surfaces. Since screws were not widely available, carpenters used large wrought iron nails to fasten latches and hinges to woodwork. Because of the danger of splitting the wood, hinges were made to cover a broad area, spreading out the nailing surface.

Such traditional forms and styles of ironwork survived in the imported and locally-made hardware used in early American buildings. Some types of hardware, like strap hinges, continued to be used in barns and outbuildings long after they had ceased to be found in the home. Among conservative groups like the Pennsylvania Germans, old traditions of wrought ironwork and decorative hardware persisted well into the 19th century.

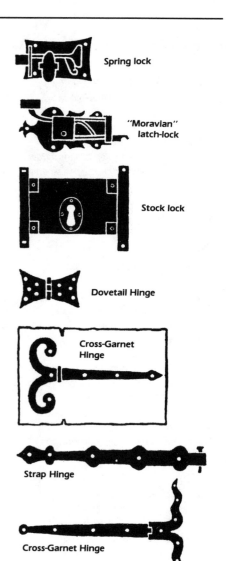

Spring lock

"Moravian" latch-lock

Stock lock

Dovetail Hinge

Cross-Garnet Hinge

Strap Hinge

Cross-Garnet Hinge

The Transition to Mass-Production

By the late 18th century, changing tastes, mass-production and new technologies had begun to supplant conservative traditions. Homeowners found earlier hardware styles crude and outdated. They demanded cheaper, more effective and less ornamented hardware. The appearance of hardware began to change.

In England, small hardware shops and the craftsmen who ran them became part of a larger system of mass-production. Though they still did much of the work by hand, shops specialized in making certain types of locks, latches or hinges. They sold their products to merchants who marketed them at home and abroad to satisfy a growing demand. Mass-marketing and an increase in output led to more standardized, less decorated hardware.

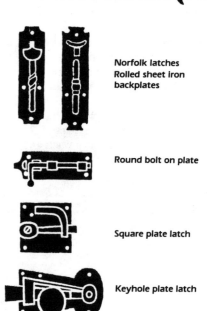

Norfolk latches
Rolled sheet iron backplates

Round bolt on plate

Square plate latch

Keyhole plate latch

The Transition to Mass Production continued

New technologies also changed the appearance of hardware. Rolling mills produced iron in large sheets, providing a cheaper raw material for lock cases and latch plates. Smiths made dies that enabled them to easily reproduce standardized parts. New methods for casting iron helped replace some wrought iron hardware parts with cast ones. Screws started to supplant nails for attaching hardware. Coupled with mass-production, technological innovation helped make hardware cheaper and more plentiful.

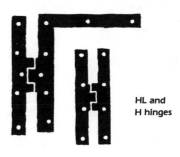

HL and
H hinges

Modern Hardware

Large-scale factory production and a series of inventions led to further changes in the appearance of building hardware. The importance of hardware as a visible decorative element continued to decline. As hardware manufacture was gradually transformed from small shop production to large scale industry, the creativity of inventors and pattern-makers replaced the craftsmanship of traditional metalsmiths.

The widespread use of cast iron butt hinges and mortise locks meant that some hardware could be concealed from view. Latches and some locks that continued to be surface mounted were embellished with cast decoration. Machines and casting made it possible to mass-produce hardware with a variety of ornament on standardized forms.

Inventors introduced a flurry of patents for butt hinges, locks, latches and nails, stimulating a growing hardware industry. Hardware that had been made with machined or cast parts could now be made entirely by these technologies. Standardized, interchangeable parts speeded and increased production.

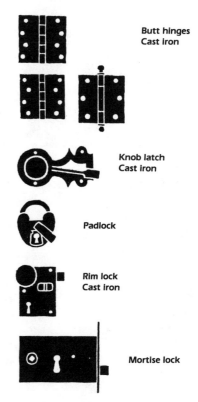

Butt hinges
Cast iron

Knob latch
Cast iron

Padlock

Rim lock
Cast iron

Mortise lock

Changing Technology: Better Locks

Warded Locks
Most locks used in early America were based on a system of wards. The interior of a warded lock contained a group of obstructions, or "box of wards", surrounding the keyhole. A key had to pass these obstructions in order to operate the lock. Only a key with a pattern of slots which matched the design of the wards could be turned in the lock. When the key turned past the barriers it lifted the tumbler, a spring-operated lever that normally prevented movement of the bolt. With the tumbler raised, the key engaged a slot in the dead bolt and slid the bolt forward or back.

The Yale Lock
Because warded locks were easy to pick, 19th century inventors attempted to produce a securer look. Linus Yale achieved the most success. In 1851 he introduced his "Magic Infallible Bank Lock" and offered a prize of $3,000 to anyone who could pick it. Later, Yale revolutionized lockmaking with his patent of the pin-tumbler cylinder lock. In his design, a flat key raised five pin-shaped tumblers in a unique pattern, allowing the key to be turned.

Baking Utensils

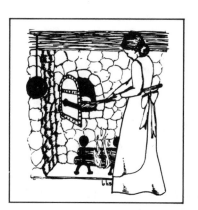

Bread Throughout History

Bread as we know it is a product baked in an oven from dough (cereal grain mixed with liquid) that has been "raised" by a leavening agent such as yeast. The ancient Egyptians were the first to bake leavened bread and to build bake ovens. By the time of Christ, western man had acquired a marked preference for raised breads of wheat and rye over the flat breads of millet, barley, and oats which had been his basic diet for many centuries.

Rye bread was favored in most European nations until about 1800. Then, influenced by France—a wheat-eating nation that ruled Europe's tastes as Rome had 2000 years before—Europe developed a great appetite for wheat bread. It was the European demand for wheat that stimulated the building of one of the largest economic empires in the history of the world —America's "Empire of Wheat."

Bread in Colonial America

In the country that would become the greatest wheatland in the world, comparatively little wheat was grown or consumed during the colonial era. The grain that sustained America for its first 200 years was corn. Within a year or two after settlement, the colonists were planting maize, using techniques of cultivating, grinding, and preparing it which they learned from the Native Americans, who had been growing it for centuries.

"Corn bread" was actually a flat cake that was baked in the embers of the fireplace on a flat stone, on the iron head of a hoe (hence the name "hoecake"), in a skillet, or in a Dutch Oven (an iron lidded kettle). Brown bread was made from a mixture of corn and rye flours. A finer, leavened bread was made by adding homemade yeast to the meal. White bread made from wheat flour did not become a staple food until America began seriously growing wheat in the 19th century.

Bake Ovens

America's first bake ovens appeared in the mid-to-late 1600's. They were simply small compartments built into the back wall of the kitchen fireplace. Later ovens were larger and were known as "Beehive Ovens," because their high domed tops resembled beehives. The "dome" extended into an adjoining room or outside the house. By 1750 ovens were being built with their openings at one side or the other of the fireplace. Sometimes, particularly among the Pennsylvania Germans, bake ovens were built entirely outside of the house either as part of an outbuilding or standing alone. Ovens were made of stone, brick, or a combination of both.

Bake ovens were usually "fired up" just once a week. The fire, built at the back of the oven, was reduced to coals after 1-2 hours. The coals were scraped in an even layer over the floor of the oven, let rest for a few minutes, and then scraped out. Generally, bread was baked first, cakes, pies, and gingerbread next, and finally, custards. The oven held its heat for many hours and was often used to dry fruit as well.

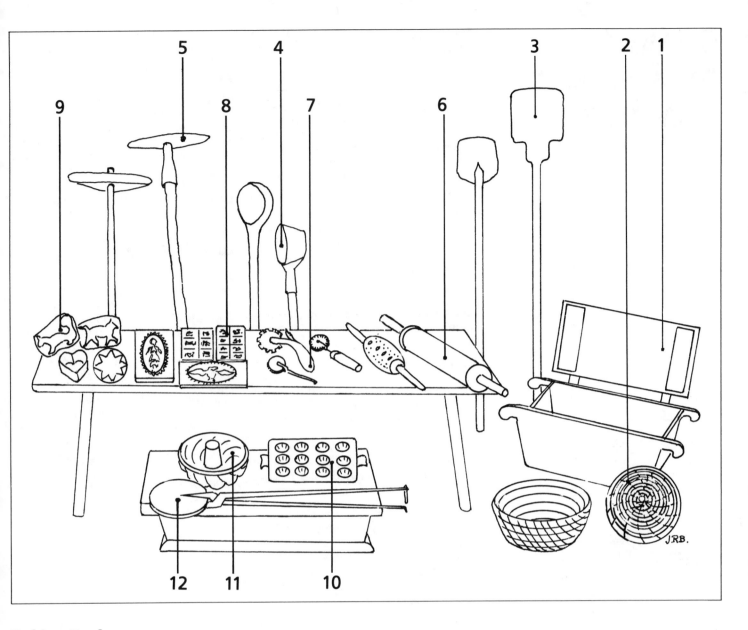

Baking Tools

1. Dough Trough:	Lidded wooden box in which bread dough was mixed and left to rise overnight before being baked.	**8. Cooky Prints:**	Known among the Pennsylvania Germans as "Springerle Molds," these carved wooden molds were for stamping rolled cooky dough with a pattern.
2. Bread Baskets:	After the dough had risen overnight, it was kneaded, divided, and placed in rye straw baskets to rise again.	**9. Cooky Cutters:**	Early cutters, made by householders and itinerant tinkers, are strips of tin crudely soldered together. Later, factory-made ones are more uniform in construction and often came in sets.
3. Peels:	Flat wood or iron "shovels" used to move baked goods in and out of the oven.		
4. Custard Dippers:	Used to pour custard into pie crusts which had first been placed in the oven.	**10. Muffin Pan:**	For baking muffins. The oldest muffin pans are made of cast iron; later ones were tin and enameled ware.
5. Ash Scrapers:	Hoe-like wood or iron tools used to spread coals over the oven floor and to scrape them out.	**11. Cake Pan:**	Cake pans often had a tube or spout in the center. This allowed the cake to bake evenly, by distributing the heat to the center of the cake.
6. Rolling Pins:	For rolling out cooky and pie dough. Some had carved designs or inlaid patterns for making fancy dough or cookies.		
7. Pie Crimpers:	Also known as "pie jaggers," these wheeled tools were used to trim, decorate, and seal pie crusts. Made of many materials, pie crimpers were often beautifully crafted.	**12. Wafer Iron:**	These were used over the hot hearth coals to bake thin, crisp wafers—a favorite confection when sprinkled with powdered sugar or rolled up and filled with whipped cream.

Basket and Broom Making

Basket Making Through The Ages

One of man's basic needs is for containers to store and carry food and possessions. Plant fibers woven into simple receptacles—baskets—are the most ancient type of container. The oldest preserved baskets are large circular grain containers found in Egypt. These date from about 5000 B.C., but the craft of basketry is certainly of greater antiquity.

Baskets have been made from a wide variety of materials: twigs, reeds, canes, rushes, leaves, grass, straw, bark, and splints (strips) of wood. Baskets have always been made using one of two basic techniques: either by coiling spiral twists of fibers such as straw into round and oval shapes or by plaiting (weaving) material such as willow shoots or oak splints into many shapes.

Baskets in America

The first settlers brought with them basket making skills which had been utilized for centuries in Europe. The Native Americans were also basket makers with an unbroken tradition going back thousands of years. The two cultures freely exchanged styles, designs, and techniques.

American baskets were made of three materials: wood, split into thin flexible splints and woven into strong, durable baskets; willow branches, woven into "wicker" baskets; and straw, coiled into basket shapes and bound together with heavy cords or strips of wood. The

Palatine Germans who settled in New York, Pennsylvania, and New Jersey, were the main group that used straw, particularly rye straw, for basketry.

Baskets of many styles and sizes were needed for a variety of domestic, agricultural, and industrial uses. Many people made basketry their chief business, while others pursued it as a sideline to their regular vocation. In the late 19th century, however, as commercial packaging—paper bags and boxes—became common, basketry as a utilitarian craft began to die out.

Broom Making

The first brooms made in America were "splint brooms," made by splitting one end of a hickory or birch sapling into thin strips. They were popular in New York and New England until well into the 19th century. Besides making splint brooms for their own use, many settlers sold or bartered them locally.

"Corn brooms" were made of layers of broomcorn (a special variety of the grain millet) wired onto a handle. By the mid-19th century, the cultivation of broomcorn and the production of "corn brooms" was a widespread industry in America. It was a seasonal occupation which took place in the fall when the broomcorn was harvested.

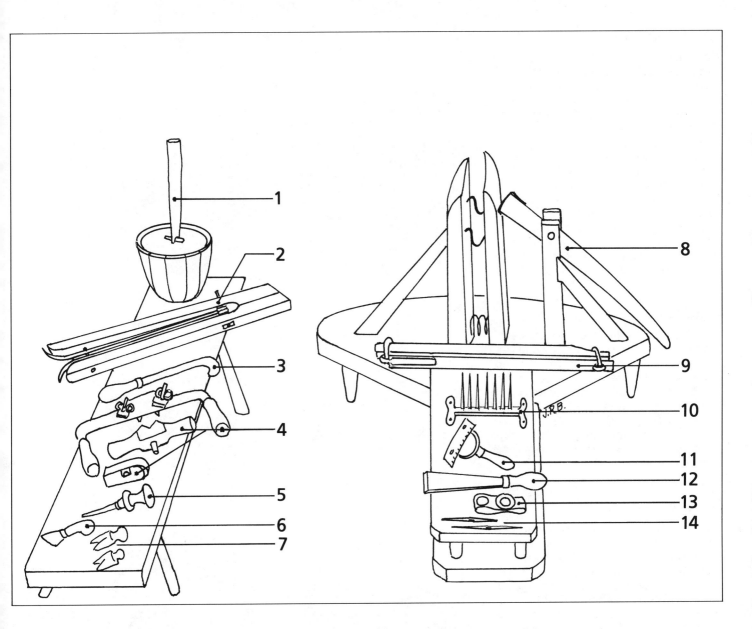

Basket Making Tools

1. Basket Mold:		While splint baskets were usually woven freehand, some basketmakers, particularly those in New England, utilized wooden molds. This mold was used to produce uniform peck-size baskets.
2. Brake:		Wet willow rods (shoots) were pulled through the jaws of this clamp-like tool placed upright on a bench to strip them of their bark.
3. Willow Knife:		Used to cut willow in the field.
4. Shaves:		Adjustable plane-like tools used to shave, trim, and smooth willow rods and wooden splints.
5. Bodkin:		Used in willow basketry to make openings in the weave for the insertion of rods.
6. Picking Knife:		Used for trimming ends of willow rods and trimming finished baskets.
7. Cleavers:		Wooden tools with four radiating cutting edges which were pushed down the length of a willow rod to split it into four skeins (strands). Skeins were used to weave small, fine baskets.

Tools to make "Corn Brooms"

8. Broom Maker's Clamp and Bench:		Homemade, lever-operated vise in which a broom was placed to be flattened and sewn. At rear of room is a later, factory-made clamp.
9. Wooden Clamp:		Simpler, less convenient device for flattening and sewing brooms.
10. Hatchel:		Used to remove the seeds from broom corn. The straw was pulled through the iron teeth.
11. Comb:		Used to "comb" the finished broom.
12. Beater:		Used to pound down the ends of the broomcorn around the handle to make it fit snugly.
13. Hand Guard:		The broom maker wore one of these on either hand to enable him to push the needle through the broomcorn.
14. Needles:		Used to sew brooms. The needle had an eye in the middle and did not have to be turned as the worker pushed it back and forth through the broomcorn.

Wicker Baskets

Several varieties of willow trees were used as basketry material, but the American green willow was the most popular. Its long, smooth, flexible branches were well-suited to weaving. In Great Britain basket willow was called "osier," and its cultivation and the making of osier baskets was a widespread and important village woodcraft. In America all sorts of domestic, farm, and market baskets were made of willow, but willow was never used as widely as splint. It was not as abundant, and it took longer to plait than wooden strips. Pictured are a deftly-woven wicker picnic basket and an open-work table basket.

Splint Baskets

The majority of American baskets were made of splint—thin strips of wood cut from sections of oak, ash, hickory, or poplar tree trunks. Soaked in water to promote flexibility, splints were woven into a great many shapes for use in the home, fields, and barn. Pictured are a small table or fruit basket with stamped decorations and a strong and serviceable egg or vegetable gathering basket.

Straw Baskets

Less common than either splint or wicker for basketry was straw. The Palatine Germans who settled parts of Pennsylvania, New York, and New Jersey were the main users of straw, particularly rye straw, for basketry. Straw was handcut with a sickle so that it would remain long and unbroken. It was then fashioned into spiral twists and coiled into basket shapes, primarily round and oval. The Indians of the American Southwest have been using this technique to make baskets for thousands of years. Pictured are two Pennsylvania German rye straw baskets: a shallow, circular bread basket in which dough was placed to rise and a bee skep or hive. Rye straw bee skeps were once quite numerous in the farmlands of Pennsylvania and New Jersey since honey was an important farm product before sugar became plentiful.

Broomcorn Machine

This is a primitive homemade machine that was used to remove the seeds from broomcorn before making brooms.

Broomcorn is a variety of the grain millet grown especially for use in broom-making. The corn was held in small bunches over the wooden edge, which acted as a guard for the operator's hands. When the drum was rotated by means of a handle, the protruding spikes pulled the seed from the end of the corn. The seed was saved to feed to fowl and cattle; the stalk was used to make brooms. This task could also be performed by using flax hetchels and curry combs, a more laborious procedure.

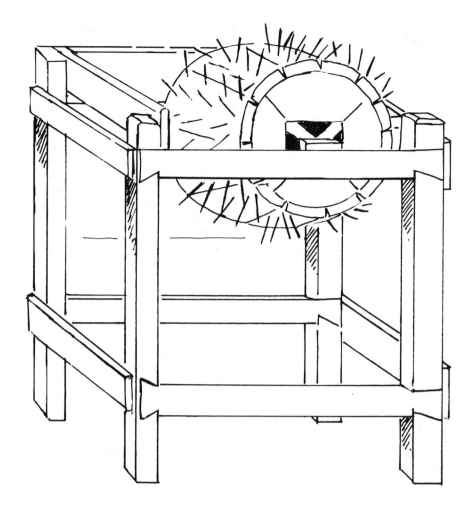

Broom-Making Machines

These hand-operated machines were used in the making of brooms from broomcorn (see broomcorn machine).

A prepared wooden handle was held in the machine so that one end protruded in front of the worker. Damp broomcorn was placed around the handle and held in place by wire, which was stored on the spool on top of the machine. The operator stepped on the round "cage" located near the floor, causing the handle to rotate and the wire to wrap around both the handle and the corn. This was repeated several times. When sufficient corn had been wired in place, the broom was placed in a special clamp and the broomcorn sewn permanently in place with twine. The ends were trimmed and the broom was placed in a rack to dry. Broom-making was an important rural industry in 19th century America. It was a seasonal occupation, rarely lasting longer than a few months in the fall when the broomcorn was ready to use.

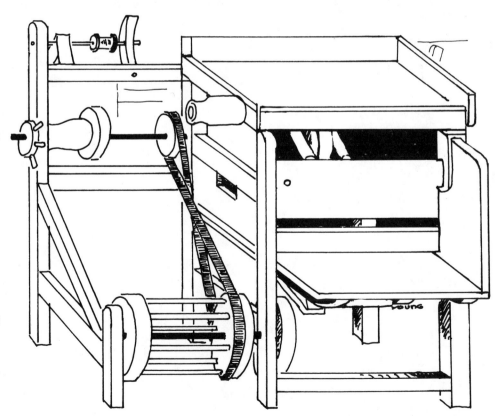

Blacksmithing

Iron: The Smith's Material

The exact time and place that man learned to make and shape iron is unknown, but historians believe that ironworking may have begun as early as 4000 B.C. in the Caucasus Mountains of Russia. Knowledge of smelting and forging iron had reached Greece and Europe by 1500 B.C., and this is the date usually given as the start of the "Iron Age" in Europe. By the 5th century B.C. knowledge of ironworking had reached Britain, ending the Bronze Age there. The Native Americans never learned to mine and smelt iron, so it may be said that the Iron Age began in North America with the coming of the first Europeans.

In colonial America, as in Europe, iron was smelted (separated from the ore) in blast furnaces fueled by charcoal. Blast furnaces were established in New England by the 1640's, and by the mid-1700's ironworks were in operation in nearly every colony. The ore was obtained from bogs and ponds or mined from just below the earth's surface with pick and shovel. Impurities were separated from the iron during the smelting process and the metal was run off into molds as "pig iron." Pig iron was suitable for being cast into stove plates, firebacks, cannon, and shot, but was too brittle to be forged by the blacksmith. Malleable wrought iron was the basic material for hand forging at the fire and was made from pig iron in an open forge called a finery, or refinery.

The Blacksmith in Europe and America

Throughout the centuries the blacksmith's function was to make tools, weapons, and to a lesser degree, works of art. During the late medieval period, the church and feudal lords—demanding decorative works and armaments—were the greatest patrons of the blacksmith, and the art of blacksmithing reached a high level of perfection during that time.

The blacksmith was certainly one of early America's most indispensable and visible craftsmen. Whether working in a large city, a small town, or at a backwoods forge on the fringes of civilization , he made tools, kitchen utensils, nails, hinges, latches, lighting devices, plow and harrow points, and wagon hardware and tires—all the objects needed for survival and comfort in the new nation.

The blacksmith has been characterized by brute strength, but surely this is unfair. Intellect, imagination, the power of visualization, and the sensitivity of the artist were needed in addition to strength to transform raw ironstock into objects of utility and beauty.

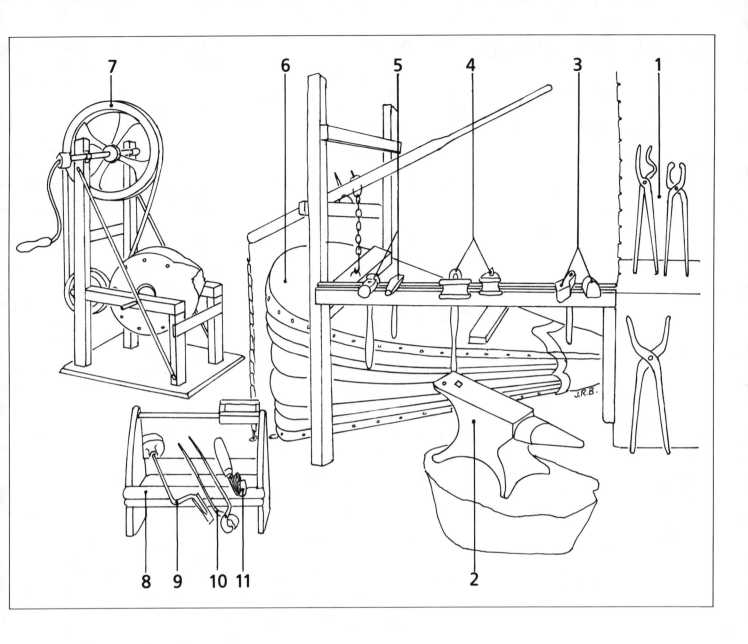

Blacksmithing Tools

1. Tongs: Used to hold hot metal as it was being worked. Many varieties were used, depending on the shape and size of the work.

2. Anvil: Indispensable in the shop, the anvil was used for everything from rough forging to delicate bending. Holes set in the anvil allowed insertion of fullers, swages, and other tools.

3. Fuller: This tool had top and bottom parts and was used for a variety of jobs. Its main function was "fullering"—a process of drawing out, or lengthening, metal by pounding it between the two parts.

4. Swage: Swages came in a wide variety of sizes and were used for rounding and "drawing" iron stock. The bottom part fit into a hole in the anvil; the top part (with the handle) was then held over the work and pounded.

5. Hammers: Came in many sizes to suit specific jobs. However, their use depended on the individual blacksmith who would normally use one favorite hammer for almost everything.

6. Great Bellows: A giant wood and leather "lung," pumped by means of a lever and chain, used to force a steady stream of air over the coals in the forge to intensify their heat output. Three flat boards connected by pleated leather form two airtight chambers. At the small end is a pipe connecting the bellows to the "tuyère," an adjustable air nozzle leading directly into the coals.

7. Blower: Hand-cranked blowers began to replace bellows in the second half of the 19th century.

8. Farrier's Box: Many blacksmiths specialized in farriery— the trade of horse and ox shoeing. This special farrier's box has compartments for tools and a box on top to hold nails.

9. Butteris: Very sharp tool used to trim horse's hooves before shoeing. Care and skill in trimming saved the horse much discomfort.

10. Hoof Parer: Also used to trim hooves. The shaping of the hoof was very important. The purpose of the shoe was merely to preserve the proper shape of the hoof.

11. Hoof Knife: Curved knife used to clean in and around the hoof and for fine shaping.

Brick Making and Stone Cutting

Brick Making

In America during the 18th century, bricks were usually made right at building sites in temporary kilns constructed of raw bricks. These kilns were known as "clamps." Clay that had been weathered (exposed to the elements for several months) was "tempered" by mixing in sand and water. It was then molded in wooden or iron forms. The molded bricks were dried for several days in the open air and then fired in the clamp to a temperature of 1800°F. The clamp was fueled by wood or coal and had a rudimentary firebox dug in the ground to distribute the heat. After firing, the entire clamp was dismantled, and the bricks, including those which had formed the walls of the kiln, were ready to be used. Those fired hottest might be used to build a chimney or bake oven; those scarcely fired, as fill in foundations.

Slate Cutting

Slate began to replace shingles as America's primary roofing material in the first quarter of the 19th century. Factors that contributed to the development of the slate industry were the completion of canals and railroads, which facilitated the transport of slate from quarries to building sites, and the need for a durable, fireproof, watertight material to roof the growing nation's buildings.

Slates were prepared at quarries by men known as "strikers" or "knappers." Large slabs were cut from the rock mass and then split into thinner slabs. Six to eight slabs could be cut from a one-inch slab by a skilled striker. After being transported to the building site by wagon, canal, or railroad, the slates were installed on the roof by men known as "slaters."

Quarrying and Stone Cutting

There were two basic techniques of quarrying stone for building: channeling and blasting. Channeling was the most common method. It involved drilling lines of holes called "channels" in the cliff face and driving wedges into the holes until a block of stone broke away from the cliff. Blasting was used on a much more limited basis. Instead of wedges, explosives were placed in the holes and set off. Although this was an effective way to separate large stone blocks from the cliff, it often caused secondary cracking and weakened the stone.

A distinct division of labor existed in the quarrying and stone cutting business. "Quarrymen" freed the stone from rock outcrops at the quarry. "Roughmasons" cut the blocks into smaller pieces and roughly dressed (finished) them. Intricate cutting and final dressing was done at the building site by men called "freemasons." Finally, men known as "layers" or "setters" constructed the building with the prepared stones.

The technological advances that industrialized America changed all three of these industries. Machines powered by steam gradually replaced hand processes and operations. Small local brick yards and quarries all over the country found it increasingly difficult to compete with large brick yards and quarries that had adopted modern methods and machine power for materials handling. In addition, growth of urban centers and improved transportation encouraged the centralization of these industries.

Brick Making and Laying Tools

1. Float: Used by brick layers to smooth mortar when building a wall.

2. Molds: Used to shape a mixture of clay, sand, and water into bricks of desired form.

3. Hoe: Used to mix mortar— a mixture of lime, sand, and water which, upon hardening, bonds bricks together.

4. Hod: Used to carry bricks from the supply pile to the building. The handle was grasped with two hands and the "head" rested on the workman's shoulder.

5. Hawk: Mortar was placed on the flat surface. The bricklayer held the hawk in one hand and used the other to smooth the mortar with a trowel and lay the brick.

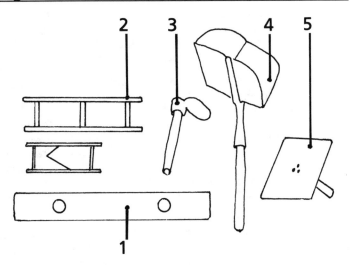

Slate Working Tools

6. Rippers: Used to remove damaged slates from a roof.

7. Choppers: Used to trim thin slabs of slate to the desired dimensions. The hook was used to punch a nail hole in the slate.

8. Drawknife: Curved, two-handled knife used to trim the slate that was used for school slates.

9. Saws: Circular and hand saws like these were used to cut slate into thin slabs at the quarry.

10. Slate Rule: Specialized tool for measuring roofing slates.

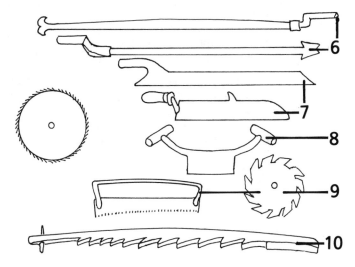

Stone Cutting Tools

11. Saw: Huge two-man saws were used to cut large blocks of stone into smaller ones. A stream of sand and water was poured steadily over the block as the saw was pulled back and forth. The abrasive sand facilitated the cutting.

12. Drill: Used by quarrymen to drill holes in the cliff face.

13. Dressing Hammers: Used by rough-masons and freemasons to carve and dress stone. These were commonly used on hard stone like granite.

14. Mallets and Chisels: Also used to dress stone, these were most often used on softer stones like limestone.

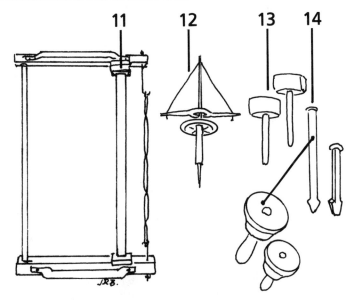

Butter & Cheese Making

Dairying in America

Butter and cheese are milk by-products used in cooking and as foods. The raising of cattle for milk and the manufacture of these goods is known as dairying.

The American dairy industry had its beginnings in 1624 with the importation of three heifers and a bull to New England from Great Britain. By 1650 cattle had been distributed to New York and Philadelphia, and the colonists were well on their way to the raising of livestock and the home production of butter and cheese.

From the early 18th century to the middle of the 19th, the making of butter and cheese was part of the daily routine of the housewife and farmwoman. Butter was churned about twice a week from September to June. (It was not made during the hottest months because high temperatures caused it to spoil.) Cheese was pressed during July and August. Butter and cheese were produced in bulk for year round family consumption and for sale and trade.

By 1850, the manufacture of dairy products was greater in America than in any other country. After 1855, large-scale factory production of dairy products was firmly established, and farm and home production of these articles gradually decreased.

Cheese

When a sour milk culture is added to milk or cream, it causes the milk to separate into curds and whey. Curd is the whitish, solid portion from which cheese is made. Whey is the thin, watery part which is pressed from the curds until the desired dryness has been achieved.

To make cheese, the curds were cut with a wooden knife and placed in a cheese drainer which rested on a tub. They were wrapped in a cheesecloth, and the whey drained through the cloth into the tub. The whey was usually mixed with cornmeal and fed to the pigs. The curds were then placed in a cheese press, a tool designed to compress the curds and remove any remaining whey.

After being pressed, the cheese was smeared with butter, wrapped in a cloth, and placed in a cheese closet to age or "ripen."

From the beginning of the 18th century, cheese and cheese dishes were standard fare in most American homes. Being high in protein, cheese was sometimes substituted for meat, and it was an important cooking ingredient. It was boiled, roasted, stewed, and toasted, and was used in hashes, ragouts, soups, and casseroles.

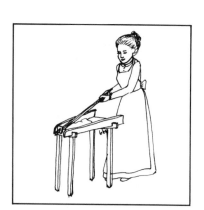

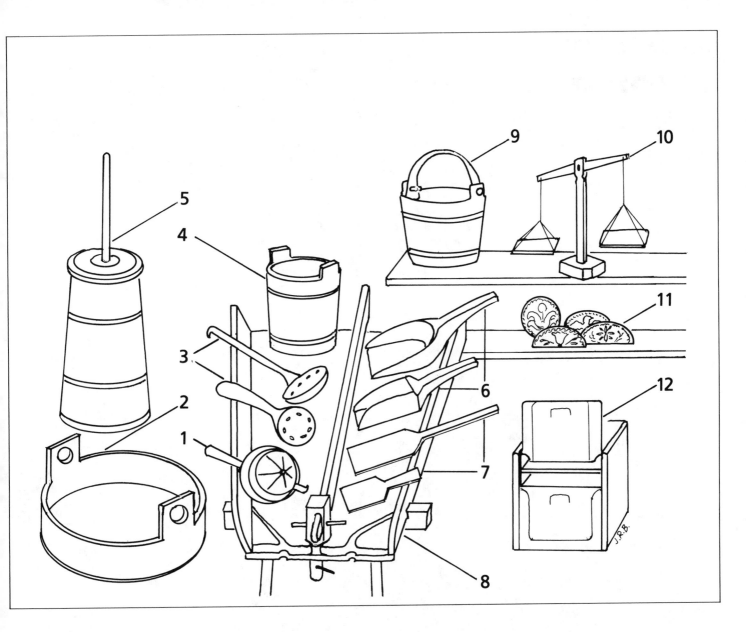

Butter Making Tools

1. Milk Strainer: Used to strain warm milk, fresh from the cow, to remove any hair or dust that might have fallen in during milking.

2. Keeler: Shallow, staved wooden tub in which milk for making butter was placed. It was set in a cool place such as the cellar or spring house until the cream rose to the top.

3. Cream Skimmers: Wooden or tin skimmers used to remove the cream from the milk daily.

4. Sour Cream Tub: Pail in which cream was kept until it soured and enough had been gathered to begin the churning process.

5. Butter Churn: Essential tool for making butter. The most common type of churn (displayed here) consists of a deep, narrow barrel with a plunger fitted through the lid. The cream was placed inside and after 30 minutes to 2 hours of steady, even churning (working the plunger up and down), globules of butter formed and rose to the top of the cream.

6. Butter Scoops: Used to remove the butter from the churn.

7. Butter Workers: Wooden paddles used to cut and press the butter after it was taken from the churn, to remove moisture clinging to it (called "working" the butter).

8. Butter Working Table: Also used to work butter. Butter was placed on the fan-shaped table and slapped with the bar pivoted at its lower, narrower end until all the moisture was removed.

9. Firkin: Wooden pail used for storage of butter.

10. Butter Scale: Used to weigh butter to be traded or sold.

11. Butter Prints: Used to imprint butter with an attractive pattern.

12. Butter Box: Used to carry butter to market.

Charcoal Burning

Charcoal was made for many centuries by burning large mounds of wood at a slow rate with as little oxygen as possible.

On a homemade ladder such as this one, the "charcoal burner" climbed to the top of the mound and lit the fire by dropping in a few chips of burning wood. One of the most common methods used to build charcoal mounds was to stack lengths of wood in vertical layers around a central pole. The cone-shaped mound was then covered with a thick layer of moist clay or earth to keep the rate of combustion at a minimum level. Burning had to be carefully regulated to prevent the wood turning into ashes instead of charcoal. Men who burned charcoal for a living lived in shacks or huts near their mounds in the woods, so that they could constantly tend them. The process took several weeks to complete.

At one time charcoal was a universal staple of frontier commerce, and many settlers turned part of their woodland into this saleable fuel. Besides being used by craftsmen such as blacksmiths and tinsmiths, huge amounts of charcoal were needed to fuel America's early iron furnaces. It is said that it took two and a half tons of charcoal to make one ton of pig iron.

Cigar Store Figures

From the earliest colonial days until the turn of the 20th century, carved wooden figures were used in America as signs for all kinds of shops.

Illiteracy was common in early America, and signs which graphically depicted the services or products of shops were a necessity. Cigar store figures are the most varied and picturesque of all trade signs and remain today as outstanding examples of American folk sculpture.

Two factors contributed to the large-scale production of these carved figures in the second half of the 19th century. The increased popularity of tobacco resulted in an increase of cigar stores, and the replacement of sailing ships by steam vessels resulted in a great number of unemployed ship figurehead carvers who turned their talents to the carving of shop figures.

Cigar store signs present us with a vivid picture of many of the personalities close to the hearts of the American people in the 19th century. You will see, hanging and standing throughout the museum, many such figures—characters of folklore and history—holding cigars, snuff, or tobacco leaves to advertise a tobacco shop.

Clock and Watchmaking

Antiquity of Clockwork

Europe's first clockmakers were the heirs to a body of technical knowledge with a long and continuous historical tradition. The history of clockwork (geared mechanisms) goes back at least to the time of the ancient Greeks who made complex models of the heavens with gear trains similar to the gear trains in the first mechanical clocks. The tradition of clockwork mechanisms for astronomical and navigational devices was carried on in the world of Islam and was eventually transmitted to medieval Europe. It remained only for the development of a device to control and regulate the movement of a train of gears to make possible the mechanical clock. This device, known as an "escapement," had been invented by the end of the 13th century.

The Clock in Europe

By 1300 there were weight-driven, automatically-regulated clocks in a number of European cities. Known as tower or turret clocks, they were huge and ponderous, with parts hammered out of iron in a blacksmith's shop. By 1500 nearly every city in Europe had at least one tower clock in a prominent public building or cathedral.

Around 1500 the mainspring was invented, and it began to replace weights as the driving power in clocks. This allowed clockmakers to begin making small, portable clocks for domestic use, as well as watches. Clocks of mature design were first produced systematically and in appreciable quantities in the German-speaking parts of central Europe. Regarded as the highest technical and artistic achievements of the age, most of the clocks produced by German clock-makers from 1550-1650 were for the wealthy. Leadership in the craft passed t[o] England and Holland after 1650, and b[y] 1700 inexpensive clocks for the middle classes were being made.

Clock and Watchmaking in America

Few, if any, clocks were made in the colonies in the 17th century. During the 18th century, the individual craftsmen making clocks in America concentrated on the production of tall-case ("grand-father") clocks. They followed English and German traditions and used only hand tools and techniques to make movements, cases, and dials.

Just after 1800, Eli Terry (1772-1852) began the first American clock factory, i[n] Plymouth, Connecticut. Terry became famous as the inventor of the "Pillar an[d] Scroll" shelf clock (the most popular clock in America for several decades), an[d] clock factories—which utilized inter-changeable parts and techniques of factory production—sprang up everywhere, though the industry was concentrated in Connecticut and Massachusetts. By 1850 large quantities of small, inexpensive clocks with spring-powered movements were being made, and "Yankee peddlers" selling New England-made clocks were a familiar sight on American roads.

American watchmaking was industrialized in the 1860's. Prior to tha[t] time, watches were handmade by individual makers who also imported an[d] repaired watches and usually sold clocks as well. The number of watches produce[d] by any one maker in America before the establishment of watch factories wa[s] very small.

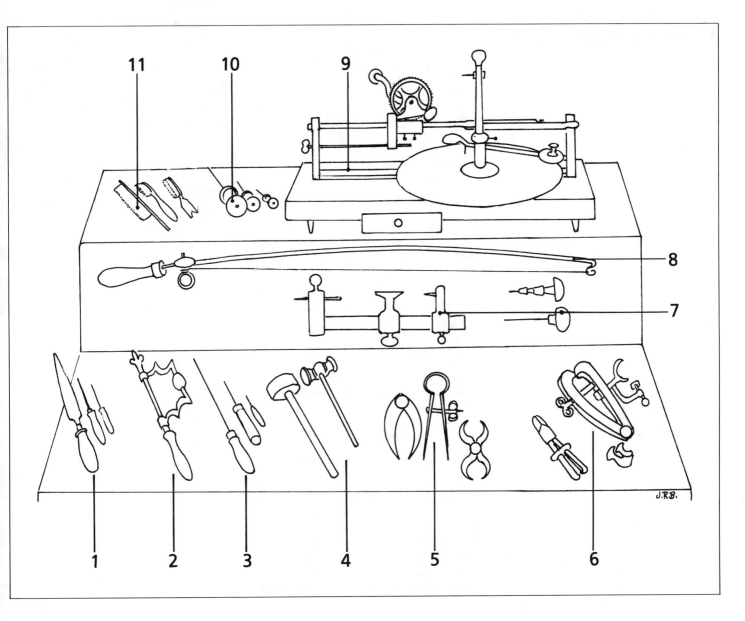

Clock and Watchmaking Tools

1. Files: Used for many purposes: rounding, cleaning, smoothing, finishing, dressing all kinds of metal parts. Dozens of sizes were needed.

2. Saws: Used to cut sheets of brass and steel, clockmakers' saws were the precursors of today's hack saws.

3. Broaches: Finely-tapered tools, round to 8-sided in section, used to ream out holes.

4. Hammers: Various kinds were used for riveting, chasing (working sheets of metal into hollow forms), and planishing (hammering metal to harden and strengthen it).

5. Marking and Measuring Tools: Compasses and dividers were used for scribing metal; calipers of different sizes were needed to take accurate measurements.

6. Holding Tools: Many special types of vises, tweezers, pliers, and tongs were needed to grasp and hold particular kinds of work.

7. Turnbench and Gravers: The turnbench, or "turns," was the forerunner of the modern metal lathe. It was used to hold metal parts while they were being shaped with steel cutting tools called gravers.

8. Bow: Used to power the turnbench. The string was twisted around a ferrule (spool) placed on one end of the metal piece being turned.

9. Wheel Cutting Engine: Hand-cranked machine (invented around 1670) for cutting the teeth in gear wheels.

10. Drills: These were powered by a bow, with the string wrapped around the spool. One point was placed in a hole in the side of a vise; the other end was applied to the metal being drilled.

11. Brushes: For cleaning watch and clock movements, which had to be kept immaculate to function properly.

Confectionery

The Art of Confectionery

Confectionery is a term that refers to the making of sweet edible substances such as sweetmeats (candied fruits), bonbons, sugarplums, hard candy, and chocolate. In the past, the person engaged in the manufacture of these articles was known as a confectioner. The delicacies were known as confects or confections, and the shop was known as a confectionery shop.

Sugar is the basis for all of the confectioner's creations; thus, this art was a natural outgrowth of the industry of sugar-refining—the process in which sugar of various grades is produced from the juice of the sugar cane plant.

By the 12th century, the cultivation of sugar cane and the knowledge of refining sugar had been brought to Europe from Asia, via Cyprus and Sicily. The Italians, Spanish, and Portuguese were the first Europeans to practice sugar-refining. The earliest historical mention of a sugar refinery in England is in 1659. By the end of the 17th century, sugar-refining and confectionery were well-established throughout Europe.

Confectionery in America

Sugar cane was found growing in the New World by the earliest Spanish and Portuguese explorers. Sugar-refining mills had been established in the Caribbean by the mid-16th century. From the islands, sugar-refining spread to the mainland of America, and the confectionery industry was soon established.

By the mid-19th century, several hundred firms in America were engaged in the manufacture of confectionery. These ranged from the village candy-maker in his one-room shop to large urban firms which made and sold hundreds of different styles of candy to markets throughout the world.

Confectionery also ranked among the foremost of the so-called "domestic arts." In the 1860's, it was considered "necessary to the economy of the household that this art form a part of every lady's education."

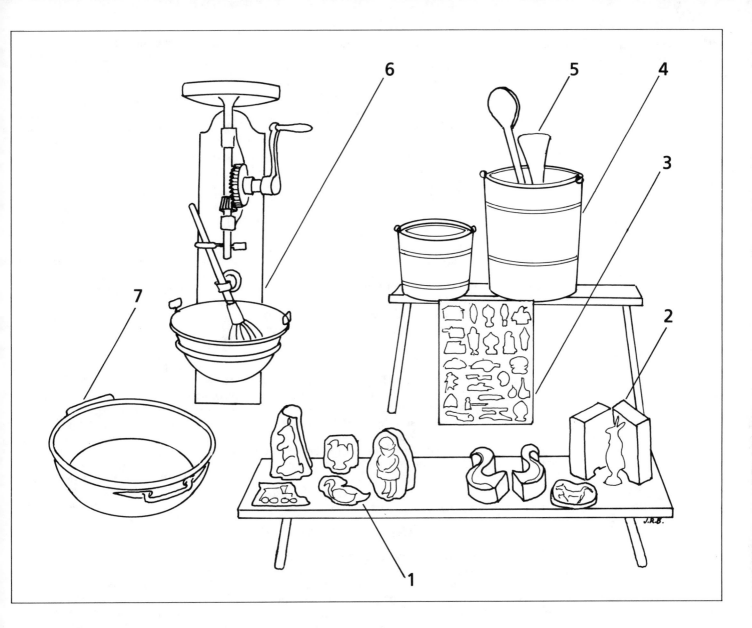

Confectionery Tools

1. Metal Moulds:	Made of zinc, iron, copper, tin, or pewter. Used to cast sugar syrup into a great variety of shapes and figures. Boiled syrup or chocolate was poured into the greased mould and allowed to cool and harden before the mould was opened.
2. Plaster Moulds:	Used in the same manner as metal moulds.
3. Plaster Forms:	Used to make hard candy figures. The form was pressed into a tray of powdered starch and removed, leaving its impression. Sugar syrup was then poured into the impression, left to harden, and removed.
4. Barrels:	Used for the storage and mixing of ingredients.
5. Paddles:	Used to stir large batches of sugar syrup, chocolate, etc., while cooking.
6. Mixing Machine:	Hand-cranked machine used for mixing large batches of syrup, caramel, butterscotch, chocolate, etc.
7. Candy Pan:	Hand-hammered and braised copper pan used for cooking batches of candy.

Coopering

History of Coopering

Coopering, the art of making wooden containers out of staves and hoops, is an ancient trade that attained a high degree of perfection very early in its history. By the first century A.D., barrels (staved containers with a bulge) were in wide use throughout the Roman Empire. Straight-sided containers such as buckets and tubs had been in use for at least 3000 years before that.

The techniques and tools of coopering, basically unchanged for centuries, were trade secrets passed down from master to apprentice.

By the 12th century, wooden barrels were the standard means of transporting liquid and dry products throughout the world, and the cooper had become one of the most indispensable of all craftsmen.

The years 1600-1850 mark the "golden age" of coopering. Following the voyages of discovery, world trade increased at a rapid rate, and there was hardly an industry which did not employ the products of cooperage either in the production or transport of goods. Coopers also made a wide variety of containers for home use, such as tubs, buckets, pails, vats, and churns.

Coopering in America

There exists no evidence that staved containers were made by the Native Americans, as neither the tools nor the end products of cooperage have been found among their material remains. It is therefore assumed that cooperage was unknown in North America prior to the European explorations.

The first cooper known to immigrate to America was John Lewes, who arrived in Jamestown, Virginia in 1608. A famous early cooper was John Alden, who came aboard the Mayflower in 1620, and who is immortalized in Longfellow's poem *The Courtship of Miles Standish*.

Coopers and their products were in great demand from the days of the earliest settlements. Many coopers came from England as indentured servants, especially to the South, and were free to practice their trade after a few years of "bound" coopering for a planter. In New England, thousands of staved containers were made for local use and for export to the West Indies.

By 1800, the products of cooperage were fifth in overall exports, and more than a third of all other exports were shipped in containers made by the cooper.

The last quarter of the 19th century saw the end of the village cooper. Good wood (especially oak) became scarce, and barrel-making machinery (introduced around 1850) had been perfected.

Types of Coopers

The Wet Cooper: The highly skilled wet cooper made barrels to hold liquid products such as beer, wine, whiskey, molasses, pitch, tar, vinegar, etc. Also known as a "tight" cooper, his barrels had to be leakproof and durable. Wet barrels were always made of oak.

The Dry Cooper: Using less exacting techniques (because his barrels did not have to be watertight), the dry cooper made barrels to hold dry products such as china, non-liquid foods, chemicals, and hardware.

The White Cooper: All kinds of straight-sided vessels such as pails, tubs, buckets, churns, and vats were made by the white cooper, for home use and industry. White coopering is the oldest branch of coopering.

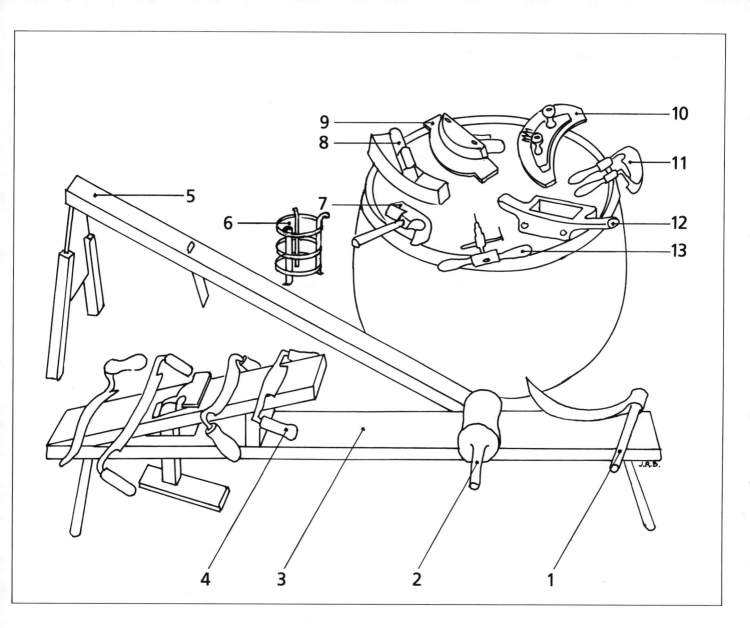

Coopering Tools

1. Froe: Used to cut the rough barrel stave from a block of wood.

2. Froe Maul: Used to drive the froe through the wood.

3. Shaving Horse: Bench on which the cooper sat while dressing (shaving) staves. The foot-operated clamp held the wood firmly so both hands were free.

4. Drawknives: Several different sizes and shapes were used to trim and shape barrel staves and heads (the wooden discs forming the top and bottom of barrels).

5. Jointer: Large upturned plane used to edge-plane barrel staves for a close fit.

6. Cresset: Iron basket in which wood was burned inside an open-ended barrel. The heat and steam made the staves pliable enough to be bent.

7. Adze: Used to even rough stave ends and to cut a bevel known as the "chime bevel" around the inside of the barrel, top and bottom. Also used to hammer down hoops.

8. Sun Plane: Curved plane used to give a final smooth surface to stave ends, after they had been assembled into a barrel.

9. Howel: Tool with a sharp blade imbedded in a wooden stock. Used to cut a channel known as the "howel channel" about one inch below the chime bevel, inside the barrel.

10. Croze: Used to cut a narrow groove inside the howel channel, into which the barrel head was forced for a water-tight seal.

11. Scorper: Sharp, rounded blade used to shave smooth the inside of the barrel.

12. Heading Swift: Shave used to dress the barrel head before insertion into the barrel.

13. Bung Auger: Boring tool used to drill the "bung-hole," which was used for filling, draining, and inspecting the liquid contents of barrels.

Pennsylvania German Decorated Chests

Chests were the main storage furnishing used in rural homes of southeastern Pennsylvania until about 1820.

Chests were owned by individual family members and were usually kept in the bedroom, where they served as benches. They were often given as gifts to adolescent girls to be used as wedding or dower chests.

Chests were painted for protective and decorative reasons. The background was often "grained"—given an overall pattern using items such as corks, combs, corncobs, brushes, leather, or feathers to apply paint in imitation of fancy woods.

The surface was then decorated with traditional Germanic motifs. Names, dates, and inscriptions often appear as well. The hinges which secure the lid to the box range from crude to superlative examples of the blacksmith's art.

The Pennsylvania German chest is one of the most distinctive manifestations of the arts and crafts of this cultural group and is a noteworthy type of painted folk furniture. It had its origins in the German and Swiss chests of the late Middle Ages. Chests like these were produced in great numbers in Pennsylvania until the first quarter of the 19th century, when popular taste began to turn away from painted furniture. They were replaced by the English chest of drawers.

Decorated Tinware

Examples of Plain and Decorated Tinware

1. Plain: The majority of early tin utensils were sold plain, with no decoration or varnish. These pieces were often decorated later at home.

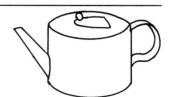

2. Pierced: Tin objects were usually pierced for practical reasons: to let the light shine from the lantern; to let the whey drain from the cheese mold; or to let the heat out from the footwarmer. Piercing was done with a chisel or punch and hammer while the tin was still flat. The holes projected from the inside to the outside of the finished object.

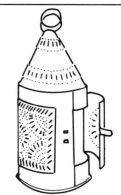

Tinware

Tinplated sheet iron, commonly known as tin, was used in the manufacture of a great variety of farm and household articles in early America. It was used mainly for kitchen and dairy utensils as well as many types of lighting devices.

American tinware was usually fashioned after practical English pottery and metal wares. The same forms were produced over and over again. Many objects made in 1790 were still being made after 1840.

3. Applied Decoration: Tinsmiths often applied additional pieces of tin as a decorative feature. Cut to a fancy shape or crimped, the pieces were soldered on after the article was formed. These articles were often unique, made to order or as a gift, and demonstrated the tinsmith's skill and ingenuity.

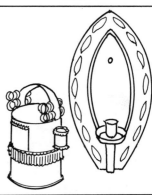

The Peddler

By 1800, the demand for tinware was so great that itinerant merchants, called tin peddlers, were hired to market it throughout the country. Five men working in a tin 'factory' could produce enough tinware to keep twenty-five peddlers supplied year round.

The tin peddler was a familiar sight on American roadways throughout the 19th century, and played an important role in the economic and social life of the country.

4. Punched: Punching was a method of decorating tinware with a design using a blunt tool (punch) that was struck with a hammer. The method was similar to piercing, but the tin was not punctured. This process was used to decorate vessels that had to be watertight, such as coffeepots.

Decorated Tinware

The desire to decorate and beautify everyday objects is readily apparent in American tinware. Tinware was not only punched and pierced in a variety of floral and geometric motifs, it was often painted in vivid colors. "Flowering" was the term used to describe the art of painting on tinware.

Painting tin was a popular pastime at home, especially in Pennsylvania, where folk art designs brought from Europe were used. In the early 19th century, the art of "flowering" became a trade, and was practiced by men and women who learned through the apprenticeship system.

5. Asphaltum: This tar-based varnish, distinguished by its brown lustre-like appearance, was used as a background for decorated tin. It was also used as a protective coat on undecorated tinware.

6. Painted: The first commercial painters, usually the tinsmith's family, used quick, precise brush strokes to produce quantities of painted tinware. When the demand became greater than could be handled by the hand-painters, stencils were substituted for free-hand designs. With stencils, decorators could repeat the same design on many pieces very quickly, thus increasing their output.

Engraving

Engraving

Engraving is the art of carving designs or figures into substances such as wood, stone, and metal. The art was practiced by many ancient people for the purpose of ornament and monumental inscription. Engraving is also the technique of printing from a carved, inked wooden block or metal plate, and in this sense is a relatively modern idea. Scholars believe that the Chinese, in the 7th or 8th century, were the first to engrave on wood for the purpose of printing. The first European prints appeared in the 14th century.

The reproduction of graphic art, using the various methods of engraving, has had a profound effect on Western civilization. The print stores and communicates information, and has played a vital role in the development of science, technology, art, commerce, religion, and politics.

Wood Engraving

The first European prints were crudely executed religious figures and playing cards, printed from carved, inked wooden blocks. "Block printing" was an invention with far-reaching effects that gave birth to the idea of moveable type and the printed book.

Wood engraving was the first graphic medium through which the American public was reached. It was relied upon to illustrate books, periodicals, and newspapers throughout the 19th century.

Copperplate Engraving

Printing from incised, inked metal plates began in 15th century Italy. This technique allowed engravers to exercise extreme finesse in their work, thus copperplate prints were far sharper, clearer, and more detailed than prints from a wooden block. Albrecht Durer and Rembrandt perfected a method of copperplate engraving known as etching. This technique uses acid (instead of carving tools) to incise the lines of a drawing into a metal plate.

Copperplate engraving was well-established in America by the mid-19th century. The technique was used to print maps, bookplates, billheads, city and scenic views, portraits, and historical subjects. Later, steel plates were substituted for copper, as thousands more prints could be obtained from a plate of the harder metal.

There are several kinds of copperplate engravings: line engravings, stipple engravings, etchings, mezzotints, and aquatints. Each type of print is the result of using a particular method to cut the lines into the metal plate.

Lithography

Invented in Germany about 1790, lithography is the process of printing from an inked stone upon which a drawing has been made with a greasy ink or chalk. It became a huge commercial success, because of its ease and speed of execution and fine results.

By 1820, several lithographic firms were in business in America, and by 1850, at least 75 firms were producing great numbers of inexpensive lithographs for the American public.

America's most prolific producer of lithographic prints was the firm of Currier and Ives of New York City. For about 50 years this firm executed millions of prints depicting virtually every aspect of America's great period of expansion and development.

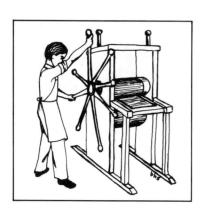

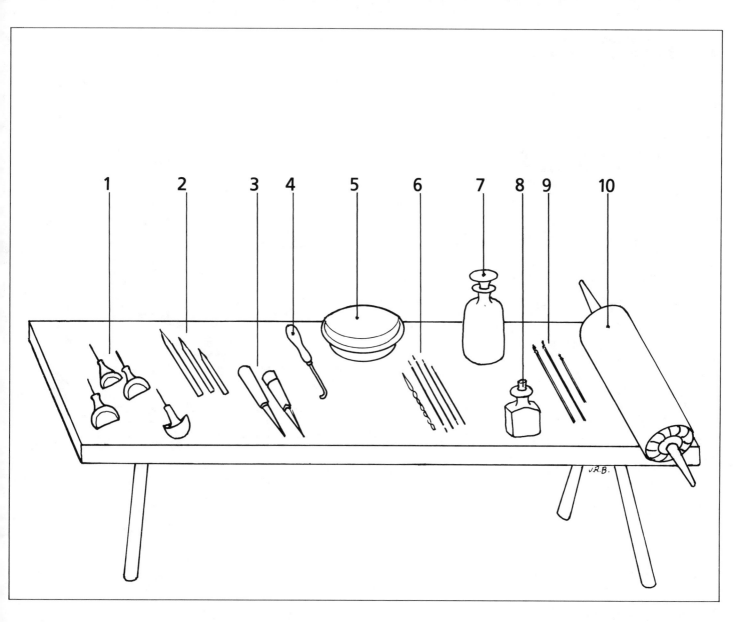

Engraving Tools

1. Gravers:
Main tool of wood and copperplate engraving. Several sizes were used to engrave the lines of the drawing into the wood or metal plate.

2. Drypoints:
Used in copperplate engraving to trace the drawing onto the metal plate and to engrave the very delicate lines.

3. Scrapers:
Used to scrape away the ridges of metal raised on either side of an engraved line by the graver as it cut.

4. Burnisher:
Used to rub down lines that were cut too deep and to burnish out defects in the plate.

5. Sandbag:
Leather cushion filled with sand on which a wood block or metal plate was rested while being engraved.

Etching Tools

6. Etching Needles:
The plate was first coated with wax, then the design was traced with these needle-like tools which cut through to the copper.

7. Diluted Nitric Acid:
Poured upon the prepared plate, acid "ate into" the copper where it had been exposed by the etching needle.

8. Stopping-out Varnish:
Used to protect ("stop out") the finer lines of the etched plate from further corrosion by the acid, which was applied in several stages to obtain the various shades of the print.

9. Stopping-out Brushes:
Used to apply the stopping-out varnish.

10. Ink Roller:
Used to apply ink to an engraved plate, which was then placed in a press and printed.

Farm Tools

Feed Choppers

Feed choppers are machines that were used to cut straw, hay, and corn into small pieces to be mixed with salt and oats and fed to livestock during the winter.

Both home- and factory-made, the feed chopper usually consisted of a narrow, shallow box with a knife blade pivoted so that it would swing down across the end of the box. The trough was filled with straw, which was held tight by an iron bar operated by a foot treadle. The knife was swung down, severing the few inches of straw that protruded over the end of the trough. After lifting the blade, the operator used a wooden or iron fork to move the straw along, and the process was repeated. It took a skilled operator about five minutes to chop up a full trough of straw.

By the middle of the 19th century, mechanical cutters with knifed wheels and feed rollers were being marketed, but most farmers preferred the simple cutting box which was cheaper and easily transportable.

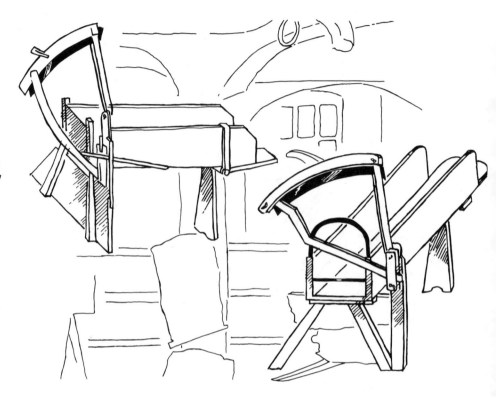

Shaving Horses

The shaving horse was used by all kinds of woodworkers to hold wood firm while it was being shaved (trimmed).

It was especially useful to coopers and shingle-makers. The workman sat astride the bench and placed a piece of wood between the clamp block and the bench top. Pushing down on the foot lever caused the clamp block to hold the wood fast, leaving the operator with both hands free to shave the wood with a drawknife.

The shaving horse was also found on many farms, being used for miscellaneous drawknife work until the late 19th century.

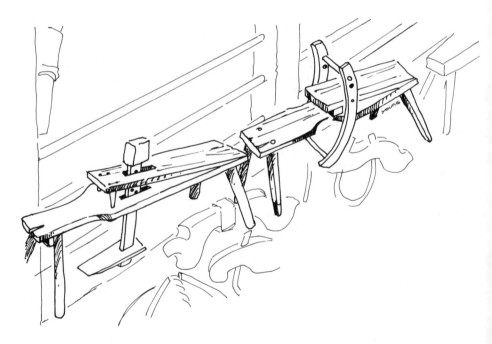

Ox Yokes

Ox yokes harnessed a pair of oxen together so they could be connected to a load to be pulled.

An ox yoke consists of the yoke itself, carved from one piece of wood, and the bows, the two steam-bent pieces of wood which fit around the necks of the oxen. Yokes were made in great numbers by farmers and local wood-workers from great curved pieces of hickory, oak, or ash. The bows were usually purchased from an ox-bow shop, and were inserted through holes in the yoke and fastened with wooden pegs. The hauling chain was attached to the large iron ring bolted through the center of the yoke. Ox yokes of this type date back to Roman times.

The use of oxen in agriculture goes back over 4000 years. They were in general use in America, for both heavy farm operations such as plowing and logging, and for pulling wagons and carts, until the first quarter of the 19th century.

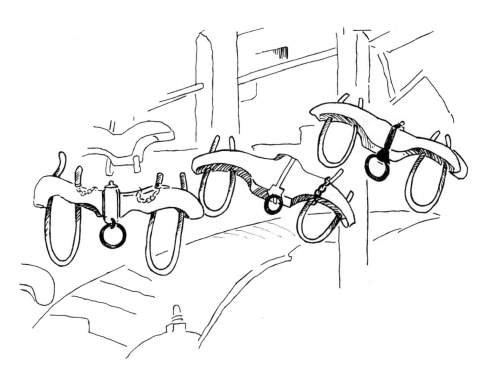

Treadmill

Horse-powered treadmills were used extensively throughout the 19th century to accomplish heavy farm jobs such as threshing, grinding grain, and sawing wood.

The rotary motion produced by the horse walking on the inclined tread was transferred to the equipment being driven by means of a belt running from the mill's flywheel to a flywheel on the machine. After 1860, steam engines began to replace "horse powers" for running farm machinery. Soon gasoline engines appeared, marking the end of horsepower as a primary method of powering America's farm machines.

Farm Tools

Fanning Mill

Also known as a grain fan or winnower, this machine was used to separate chaff (husks, or hulls, of seeds) from grain.

Inside the circular wooden casing are four wooden blades mounted on a shaft. These were turned by means of a handle on the outside of the box, creating a continuous blast of air through the box. The grain and chaff mixture was fed into the hopper on the top. As it fell through the draft, the lighter chaff, dust, and straw were blown out of the open end of the box and the heavier grain fell into a container placed below.

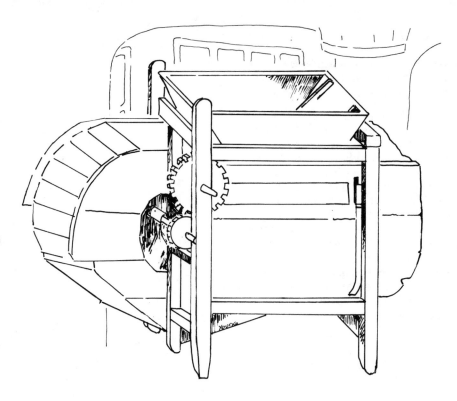

The ancient method of winnowing (separating chaff from grain) was to toss threshed grain into the wind. The wind blew away the chaff and the grain fell back to the earth or barn floor. Mechanical winnowers were invented in Holland in the 18th century and were in use in America by the beginning of the 19th century.

Gum Tree Boxes

Also known as gum boxes or simply gums, these cylindrical wooden containers were used as all-purpose bins around the home and farm.

They were made from the trunks of Black Gum trees, which almost always become hollow with age. The trunk was sawn in sections, the remaining dead wood removed from the inside, and boards were pegged to the bottom of each section. The resulting sturdy containers were used for all kinds of liquid and dry storage in the stable, barn, and home.

Farmers sometimes made their own gum boxes, but usually they were purchased from the local cooper (barrel maker). They were more commonly found in the southern states, where gum trees were plentiful. The term gum later came to mean any vessel made from the trunk of any tree.

Horse Drawn Hay Rakes

Horse drawn hay rakes were used to gather cut hay into wide rows prior to being forked onto the hay wagon and hauled to the barn for stacking.

Rakes were drawn by one horse and guided by a driver who walked behind, grasping the two handles extending back from the main beam. Introduced into hay harvesting in the early 19th century, horse drawn rakes were a great improvement over the hand rakes which had been used for centuries, being faster and more efficient. Two types of horse drawn rakes are exhibited: the Hay Collector, which had only one row of teeth; and the Revolving Hay Rake, which had two sets of teeth mounted on opposite sides of the main beam.

Horse drawn hay rakes were used well into the 20th century, until they were replaced by modern mowing machines.

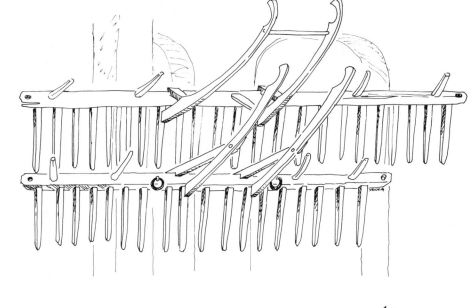

Clover Header

Clover headers were used to harvest red clover, a popular feed crop in America.

This machine was drawn by one horse and guided from the rear by a man or boy. As the header was pulled through the crop, the heads of the clover stalks were broken off by the sharp "fingers" and thrown back into the box. The operator could raise or lower the fingers according to the growth of the clover. When the box was filled, the clover was deposited in piles in the field and allowed to dry. It was then hauled to the barn to be threshed.

This type of harvesting machine was brought to America from Europe, where it had been in use for 2000 years. Red clover, noted for its quick growth, was imported into this country from England in the 18th century.

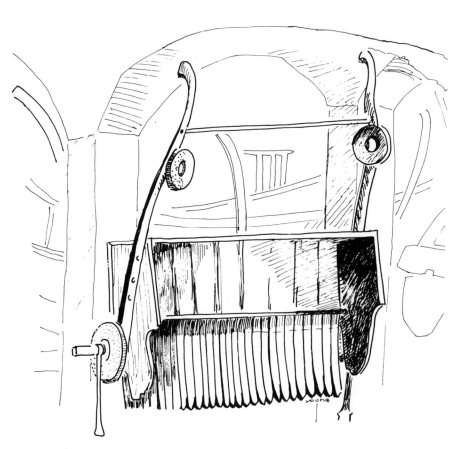

Files and File Making

The File in History

The file has been used since pre-Roman times to reduce metal and other surfaces. The ancient Assyrians, Egyptians, Chinese, and Greeks all made files, either with parallel or cross-cut grooves for metal working or with round dents (the rasp) for reducing wood. Copper and brass files were made as early as 1500 B.C.; the oldest iron file on record was made by Assyrians in the 7th century B.C.

By the 12th century the art of cutting files had reached a high level of technical expertise. A German monk of that century left detailed records describing two methods of cutting and hardening files. Fifteenth century manuscripts show file makers at work and illustrate both single- and double-cut files. Techniques of file making are considered to have reached perfection in 16th and 17th century Europe.

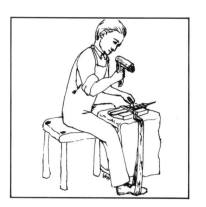

Until the introduction of machinery, file making was a highly specialized hand process. The methods and tools of file makers changed little for centuries. Roman files have been dug up in England, and differ little from files made a thousand years later.

Files were made square, round, half-round, flat, oval, and triangular. They ranged in size from mere inches to over four feet in length. There were three kinds of teeth cuts—single, double, and rasp—and about ten levels of fineness for each cut. Used in many

trades, on wood, bone, ivory, horn, leather, and all metals, the file is one of man's most basic and indispensable tools.

File Making in America

Until the mid-19th century, practically all the files used in America were imported from Sheffield, England, the center of the industry in Europe. The first American file factory was established in the 1820's in Pittsburgh. In 1845, an Englishman named John Rothery began manufacturing files in New York, and a number of other concerns soon entered the field.

Labor- and time-saving machinery was introduced in the third quarter of the 19th century, quickly putting an end to the old methods of making files. Only a few craftsmen continued to hammer them out by hand for half a century longer.

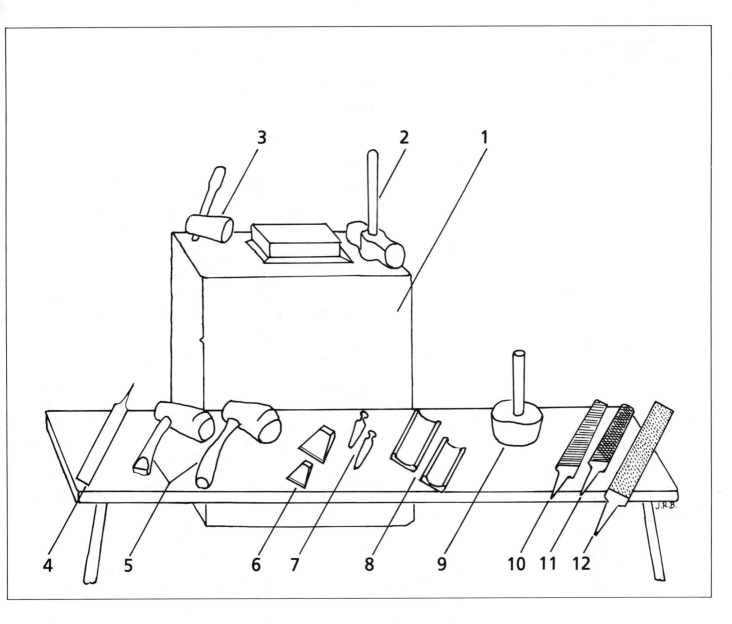

File Making Tools

1. Anvil:	A steel block embedded in a large stone sunk into the floor for stability. Used for pounding steel bars into the shape of a file and for cutting teeth in the blank.
2. Striking Hammer:	Two-handed hammer used to form hot steel bars into the shape of a file.
3. Forging Hammer:	One-handed hammer used along with the striking hammer. One worker held the steel bar on the anvil with tongs and struck the bar with this hammer, alternating blows with the man wielding the much larger, heavier striking hammer.
4. Blank:	Piece of steel formed into the final shape of the file. After softening, it was ground smooth and was ready for the file-cutter.
5. Hammers:	Specialized hammers ranging in weight from a few ounces to 8 pounds, having most of the weight concentrated at the striking end. Holding the hammer near the head, the file-cutter struck the chisel or punch at a rate of 60 to 100 times per minute, each blow forming a groove, or tooth, in the file.

6. Chisels:	Ranging in width from ½ to 2 inches; used to cut the grooves in files.
7. Punches:	Used to cut the individual teeth on rasps.
8. Lead Cushions:	Placed between the anvil and file to prevent damage to the newly-raised teeth when the file was turned over to cut the second side.
9. Lead Maul:	Used to straighten the file after the cutting was finished. Heavy enough to flatten the file, but soft enough not to damage the teeth.
10. Single-Cut File:	Parallel grooves cut at an oblique angle across the file.
11. Double-Cut File:	Two courses of grooves, cut at right angles to each other, forming pointed teeth.
12. Rasp:	Individual teeth made with a punch in staggered rows.

Fishing and Trapping

Fishing

The methods of catching fish in early America differed little from those used throughout the world since antiquity. Fish were caught with a hook and line, with a spear or "gig," and with a net or seine, depending on the fish being sought and the conditions. The waters everywhere teemed with fish, and commercial "fisheries" located on rivers and bays throughout the country supplied Americans with all manner of fish. In the cities fresh fish—notably herring, mackerel, cod, and salmon—were sold at fish markets or "hawked" in the streets. Fish that was not sold fresh to customers and dealers was cured with salt or smoked for later sale.

The most abundant and important food fish in Pennsylvania was shad. Throughout the first half of the 19th century at hundreds of fisheries on the Delaware and Susquehanna Rivers, hauls were immense. Sometimes thousands of shad were taken in one night. Families living on or near the rivers caught enough fish to last through the winter, and from the towns and cities people came to buy and trade "city goods" for fish. Other common food fish were trout, wall-eyed pike, pickerel, catfish, and black bass. The bass was introduced into Pennsylvania's waters in 1870 from the Potomac. It flourished and rapidly became a favorite food and game fish.

By the third quarter of the 19th century, the enormous hauls of earlier years had begun to decline. Pollution, dams, land development, and illegal and destructive fishing techniques led to the depletion of major fish populations. Conservationists have attempted to restock and restore the great rivers, but the damage has been done; never again will America's waters yield the enormous returns that they did for its first 250 years.

Steel Traps

It is not known when the double-spring steel trap was invented, but it was being used as early as the 16th century in Europe. Predominant were the medium-sized traps needed to capture pests around the farm and to catch valuable fur-bearing animals of the forest.

17th century records preserved in Massachusetts and Virginia testify to the use of steel traps by the colonists, and by the early 18th century steel traps were in widespread use by professional trappers. Traps were handmade by blacksmiths until well into the 19th century, and on the frontier smiths were kept busy making and repairing traps for trappers and fur companies.

The Fur Trade

The beaver trap was the foundation of a great financial empire in early America—the fur trade. The European breeding grounds of the beaver had been depleted by the 17th century because of the great demand for pelts to make top hats worn by gentlemen. A new source of pelts was needed, and America became that source. The trapping of beaver was an important American wilderness enterprise for over 150 years. Colossal fortunes were made in the fur trade, and trappers working independently or for large firms like the Hudson Bay Company and the American Fur Company did much of the basic pioneering that led to the settling of the American West.

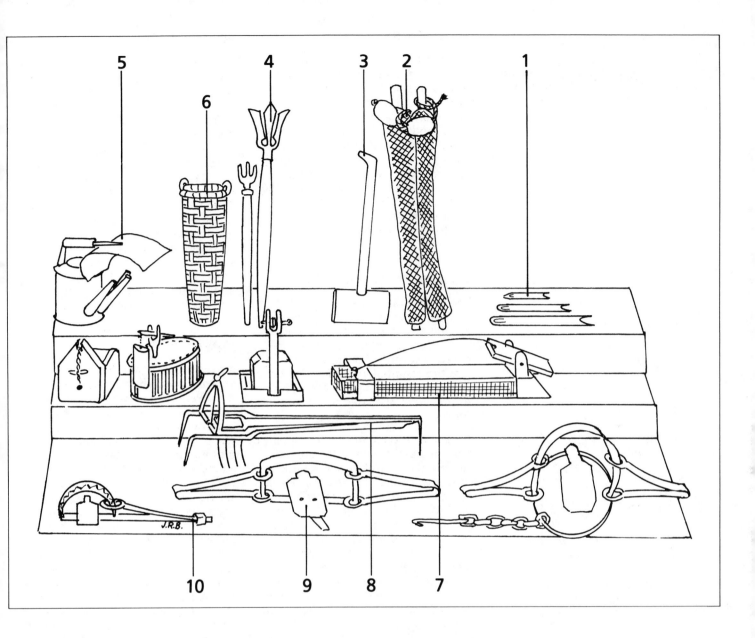

Fishing Tools

1. Shuttles:	Used to weave and repair fish nets.
2. Fishing Net:	The stakes were driven into the beach along the low water line. As the tide rose, fish passed over the net to feed in the shallows. When the tide receded, they were caught in the net.
3. Mallet:	Used for ice fishing. The fisherman located a fish through the clear ice. He then struck a blow on the ice which stunned the fish. A hole was cut in the ice, and the fish was secured.
4. Gigs:	Pronged spears used for spearing fish in shallow water. Gig fishing most frequently took place at night.
5. Gig Light:	This 3-burner kerosene lamp was used for night fishing. The shield deflected the rays from the operator's eyes and caused more light to shine on the water.
6. Eel Trap:	Inside the splint basket is a smaller basket with an opening at its tapered end. This opening allowed the eel to swim into the lower portion of the large basket but prevented its escape.

Animal Traps

7. Mouse Traps:	Many kinds of ingenious wooden mouse traps were manufactured or homemade. Some of these devices killed mice, but most trapped them alive.
8. Mole Trap:	When the trap was set, the trigger partially blocked the mole's tunnel. The sharp tines were poised above the tunnel, and when the mole passed by, the tines sprang down.
9. Animal Traps:	Typical of the steel traps used in the fur trade, these were used to catch not only beaver, but also foxes, lynxes, martens, muskrats, possums, and even wolves. The springs were depressed, allowing the jaws to be spread open and set. When an animal stepped on the "pan," the springs released, allowing the jaws to snap shut and trap the animal.
10. Sawtooth Rat Trap:	These traps, of English origin, operated on exactly the same principle as the much larger animal traps.

Fruit Preservation

Fruit Preservation

Two methods of preserving fruit for year-round eating were used before refrigeration: drying and canning. Great quantities of apples, peaches, plums, and grapes were harvested, dried, and stored, to be prepared and eaten in many different ways throughout the year. The process of canning—sealing food in glass jars using pressure and high heat—was invented in 1809 and by the 1830's was widely used by housewives to preserve fruit in the form of marmalades, preserves, and jellies.

Apples and Apple Parers

The apple was a staple in the diet of early Americans, and was grown and dried in greater quantities than any other fruit. Dried apples were prepared in countless ways, and the fruit was the essential ingredient for cider (the national drink) and applejack. Apples were also used to fatten pigs for slaughter.

The preparation of the winter's supply of dried apples was one of the annual autumn chores on farms, like husking corn. It was usually done in the kitchen by women, with now and then a "paring bee" to turn the dull task of paring uncounted numbers of apples into a social event. Women's nimble fingers made quick work of the paring, but there were also men—bachelors, widowers, and others—who had to provide themselves with winter rations of dried apples. With fingers too clumsy

and stiffened by heavy farm work to make quick work of paring, they must have early put their wits to work to find an easier and speedier method. Thus the mechanical apple parer—one of 19th century America's most useful and ubiquitous "gadgets"—came into being. The earliest paring machines were very simple and made entirely of wood. They consisted of a fork on which the apple was impaled, and a crank to rotate it while a hand-held knife did the paring. The first patent for a wooden parer was obtained by Moses Coates of Pennsylvania in 1803. Improvements followed one another in quick succession, and by the 1850's cast iron parers had appeared. By the 1870's a large industry in the manufacture of cast iron apple parers had sprung up.

Apple Butter

It may be safely said that apple butter is an American dish; more specifically, that it is a Pennsylvania German one. In Pennsylvania, the making of apple butter was a regular autumn occurrence. The process—beginning with the pressing of the cider (essential ingredient of apple butter) and ending with the "putting up" of the butter in earthenware pots or glass jars—took about two days to complete. In many cases, the making of apple butter was an excuse for a neighborhood frolic—a time for eating, drinking, dancing, and socializing during the 10-13 hours of continuous stirring of the apple butter required by most recipes. Events such as this, though not without long hours of hard work, were a welcome change in the routine and often monotonous life of the farm family.

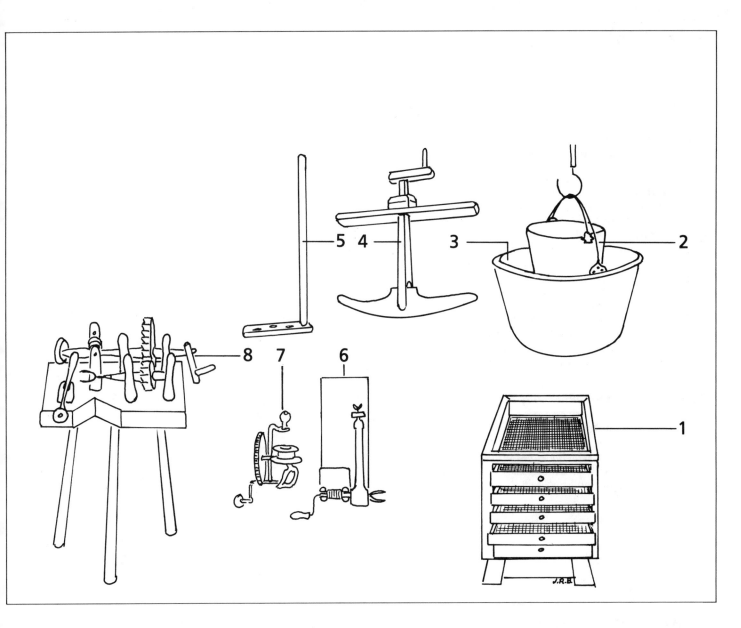

Apple Preserving Tools

1. Apple Dryer:	Fruit was sliced and placed on the sliding wire mesh trays, to be dried in the sun.
2. Preserving Kettle:	Kettle in which fruit and sugar were boiled before being "put up" (canned) in hot jars.
3. Apple Butter Kettle:	Large kettle used for making apple butter, a Pennsylvania German specialty. Cider, apples, and spices were placed in the kettle, which was suspended over an open fire, and boiled for several hours.
4. Apple Butter Stirrer:	Wooden paddle used to stir apple butter as it cooked. A handle up to 15 feet long was attached to the crank to protect the operator from the fire and the spitting and sputtering of the apple butter. When the handle was turned the paddle rotated through the apple butter.
5. Apple Butter Stick:	Long-handled wooden stick usually made of hickory, used to stir apple butter.
6-8. Apple Parers:	Designed to simplify and speed up the task of peeling large quantities of apples. **6.** A basic wooden parer of the simplest kind. **7.** An example of the cast-iron parers of the late 19th century. **8.** A complex geared wooden parer standing on three legs; made about 1800

Cider Making

Knob Mill

The knob mill was used to crush apples to prepare them for pressing in the cider press.

It was powered by a horse harnessed to the end of the long pole and walking around in a circle. Fresh apples were loaded into a hopper, which was hooked onto the end of the mill near the rollers. The apples were crushed between the rollers and fell into the trough on the other side. The crushed apples were called "pomace." As the trough filled, the pomace was pulled to the other end with wooden rakes. It was usually left overnight before being packed into the cider press. It took approximately three hours to grind a cartload of apples with the knob mill.

By the middle of the 19th century, cast iron apple grinders were being commercially manufactured. They worked much faster and ground the fruit to a finer pulp, which yielded up to 30 per cent more cider than apples ground by the wooden knob mill.

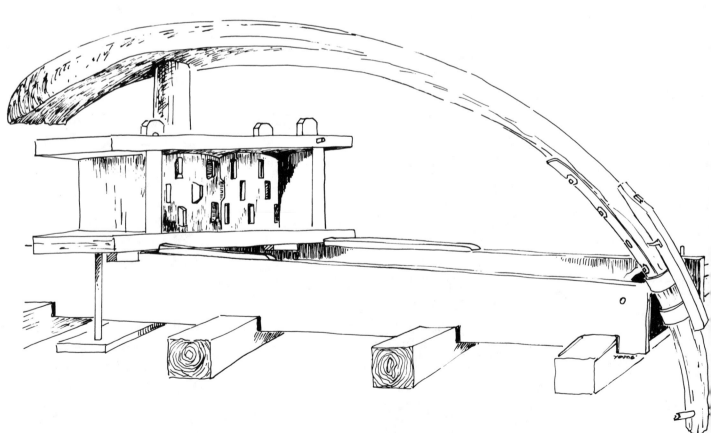

Beam Cider Press

Crushed apples squeezed in a press like this Beam Press from upper Bucks County yielded great quantities of cider, one of early America's most important beverages.

A box made of vertical slats situated on a platform under the beam was alternately filled with layers of crushed apples and clean straw. These layers were called "cheeses." The highest cheese was covered with planks and blocks of wood to bring it up to the level of the beam. By turning the big screw, the beam was lifted off its supports (which were then removed) so that it could be slowly lowered onto the apples. The layers of straw acted as a filter, keeping the pulp in the box and allowing the juice to flow down into a container. Stones might be added to the top of the beam to increase the downward force.

While all parts of America relied on cider as a beverage, Pennsylvania and New Jersey were particularly suited to commercial apple growing and cider production.

Screw Cider Press

This large press, operated by turning the two wooden screws, was used to press the juice from crushed apples, in order to make cider.

Apples were layered with straw in "cheeses" on the bed of this press in the same manner as they were on the beam press above. Sometimes the cheeses were separated by slatted spacers made of wood that would allow the cider to flow more freely. In the beam cider press the screw simply held the beam up. In this press, the screw actually drew the roof and beam of the press right down on top of the cheeses with a tremendous force, squeezing out the juice which then ran down a channel into a barrel. Presses of this size were usually used to make cider on a commercial basis.

Abundant quantities of cider were consumed by American families because cider was one of the few beverages that was easy to make and easy to store. Cider could be boiled to produce apple juice, drunk fresh as sweet cider, allowed to ferment into a bubbly alcoholic beverage like beer called hard cider, or distilled to make applejack.

General Store

The country store was a unique economic and social institution in 18th and 19th century America. It supplied the local community with the materials needed for a wide variety of domestic and farming tasks and functioned as a center of social life. It also served as a community message center, parcel room, informal bank, gossip center, reading room, and as a political forum for the "cracker barrel philosophers" who gathered there.

The Merchants

Country store merchants formed a distinct class of society and did much to nourish the growth of trade and commerce in America. A storekeeper often served as town clerk, justice of the peace, and postmaster. He was an important figure in the community, and his store brought civilization to the people it served, influencing standards and values as television and advertising do today.

The Merchandise

The merchandise reflected the needs, crafts, and customs of rural America. The stock of a typical mid-19th century store included textiles, sewing notions, dress accessories, men's wear, medicines and groceries, hardware and tools, china and crockery, dry goods and kitchen utensils.

Goods were displayed on shelves and counters, and were hung from the ceiling. In the 1830's, printed labels, boxes, and packages were used for the first time. Paper bags and canned goods appeared in the 1860's.

Much of the storekeeper's time was spent in acquiring merchandise. Stock was ordered from dealers, bought from traveling salesmen, or purchased on semi-annual trips to the nearest city.

Transacting Business

The system of bartering, or trading by exchanging one commodity for another, is one of man's most ancient and fundamental methods of transacting business. It was a basic economic factor in the establishment of commerce in America. From the trading posts of the 17th century to the country stores of the 19th, barter was more often than not the medium of exchange between a merchant and his customers. Little 'hard cash' passed between a country storekeeper and his customers. The merchant accepted almost any item in exchange for his merchandise, including foodstuffs such as butter, cheese, and eggs. Two other methods of conducting business were the extension of credit by the merchant, and the promise of labor on the part of the customer.

The Feasterville General Store

The Feasterville General Store was acquired by the Mercer Museum in 1961. It had been in business for over 125 years at the intersection of the Bristol and Philadelphia Roads, in Southampton Township, Bucks County, Pennsylvania.

From 1828 to 1901 it was owned and operated by the Knight family. The Merrick and Lennon families continued the operation of the store until 1957.

The present appearance of the store, including shelves and counters, dates from 1865-1870, when it was remodeled.

Glassblowing

Glassmaking

During the Bronze Age, people made use of a natural glass called obsidian to make weapons, tools, ceremonial objects, jewelry, and mirrors.

Glass as we know it is made of a silica, usually in the form of sand; alkalis such as potash and soda, for flux; and metallic oxides such as copper, cobalt, and manganese, for color. When subjected to intense heat, these ingredients flow together and emerge from the furnace in a molten or "plastic" state capable of being shaped. It is unknown just when glass was first made artificially, but scholars believe that glass beads may have been produced in Mesopotamia as early as 2500 B.C.

By 1500 B.C. the Egyptians were making colorful and decorative glass vessels for perfumes and unguents. These were made by tediously winding threads of molten glass around a sand "core" and then smoothing the surface by rolling it on a smooth stone. After the glass object cooled and hardened, the sand core was removed. Glass vessels produced using this slow and laborious process were limited in number and probably available only to the nobility. It was not until the invention of glass blowing that glass became somewhat more available to the middle and lower classes.

The invention of the blowpipe, attributed to Syria between 100 B.C. and 100 A.D., revolutionized the art of glassmaking. The Romans became skilled glass blowers, and by the 3rd century glass articles were in common use throughout the known world. By the 16th century, Venice had become the center of glassmaking in the West. In the late 17th century, the English made a singular contribution to the art: the development of colorless lead

or flint glass, which was superior in quality and brilliance to any other type.

Glassmaking in America

The 17th century saw the start of glassmaking in America, but information about this period is scant and no known specimens survive. In the 18th century, the industry was stabilized and expanded by major manufacturers such as Wistar, Stiegel, and Amelung. To fill the needs of a rapidly growing nation, production was focused on window glass, bottles, and utilitarian vessels.

By 1876, there were over 250 glasshouses (factories) in America and three major technical developments had occurred: the use of full-size molds to form and decorate glassware, the invention of mechanical pressing, and the successful production of flint glass.

The Dorflinger Glass Works

Christian Dorflinger, one of the great glassmakers of America, established a glass house near White Mills, Pennsylvania, in 1865. For 56 years he produced superlative glassware, built an international reputation, and profoundly influenced the industry. Many of the glass-cutting shops in the country preferred Dorflinger crystal for its quality and brilliance.

The tools, glassware, and equipment in the museum collection were acquired from the Dorflinger factory, which closed in 1921.

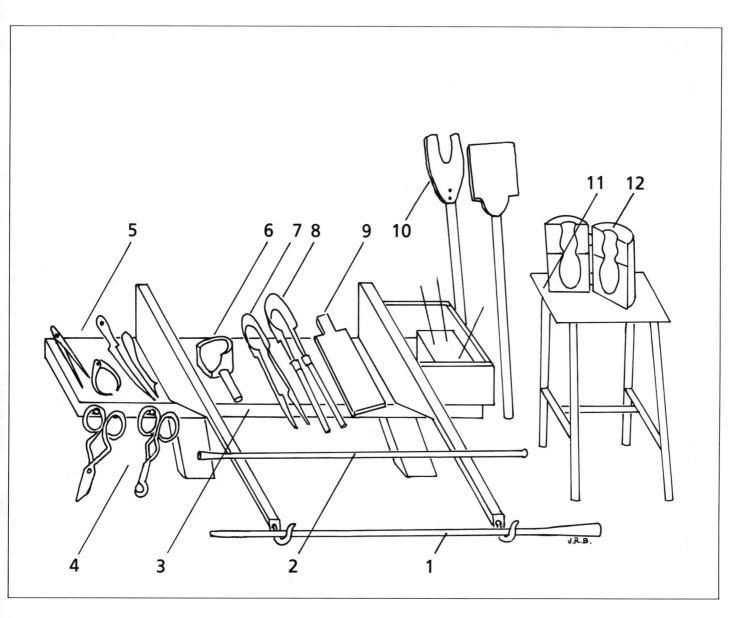

Glassblowing Tools

1. Blowpipe or Blowiron: The glass blower picked up a gather (blob) of molten glass on the end of this iron pipe by inserting it into the furnace and twisting it. He then blew through the other end to inflate the molten glass with air.

2. Pontil or Ponty Rod: This solid iron rod was fused to the base of the glass object for finishing by hand. When the piece was completed, the rod was freed with a brisk rap, leaving a scar known as a pontil mark.

3. The Chair: Wooden bench on which the gaffer (master-blower) sat while shaping a blown glass object.

4. Shears: Used to trim excess glass during the shaping process.

5. Gauges and Calipers: Used to measure the diameter and height of glass objects during the shaping process.

6. Block: Used in the early stages of manipulation to give a symmetrical form to an inflated gather on the end of the blowpipe.

7. Pucellas: Iron or steel tongs used in nearly all shaping operations. Called "the tool" in the trade.

8. Woodjack: Used in the same manner as the pucellas. The wooden prongs were replaced when they became too charred for further use.

9. Battledore: Wooden paddle to flatten the bottom of blown glass objects.

10. Wooden Fork & Shovel: Long-handled tools used to place a finished glass object in the annealing (cooling) oven.

11. Marver: Steel stand on which the gather was rolled to give it a uniform thickness and symmetry before blowing.

12. Iron Mold: Used in making blown-molded lamp chimneys.

Gunsmithing and Weapons

Firearms: 1300 to 1700

The European discovery that the explosive energy of gunpowder could be used to hurl objects apparently came from Arab writings which described mixtures of saltpetre, charcoal, and sulfur used by the Chinese for pyrotechnics. The first portable firearms—crude "hand cannons"—were in use by the 14th century. During the next 500 years the mixtures of gunpowder varied little. Until the 19th century the creative and technical skills of gunsmiths were directed towards improving methods for igniting the powder. This evolution closely paralleled man's progress in mechanical aptitude and manufacturing capacity.

Regardless of the type of ignition system used (matchlock, wheellock, or flintlock), martial firearms were usually heavier and more cumbersome than weapons for sport. Sporting and hunting weapons frequently displayed elegance coupled with innovative design, for they were made to order for affluent patrons. Surviving early weapons of this nature indicate that Europe's first "armorers" were heirs to a long tradition of fine metal working.

Guns and Gunsmithing in America

The American colonists were the greatest weapon-using people of that epoch in the world. The gun furnished daily food, it helped its owner maintain possession of his home and property, and it enabled the young nation to win its wars for possession of a continent. Frequently laboring under primitive conditions with the most basic hand tools, the early American gunsmith fashioned and repaired a complex and vital commodity needed for survival.

Gunsmiths were established in the British colonies by 1630. During the 17th and 18th centuries, many English, German, Swiss, Irish, and Scottish smiths emigrated to America, bringing with them the technical skills they had learned in the Old World and the many hand tools and few machines with which they pursued their craft. There were, it is estimated, about 2000 practicing gunsmiths in British America when the War for Independence broke out. Possibly two-thirds of these embraced the patriot cause, and they produced large numbers of martial firearms under contracts from Congress, Committees of Safety, and their own states.

After the Revolution, the need to equip a national defense force prompted the establishment of two national manufacturing armories—one at Springfield, Massachusetts and one at Harper's Ferry, Virginia. The fledgling industry attempted from the beginning to achieve consistency in design and quality. By 1800 water-powered machinery had been developed, and with the U.S. Model 1816 Musket, standardization and interchangeability of parts had been realized. In 1861-62, the Springfield Arsenal produced 3/4 of a million identical rifled muskets for use in the Civil War.

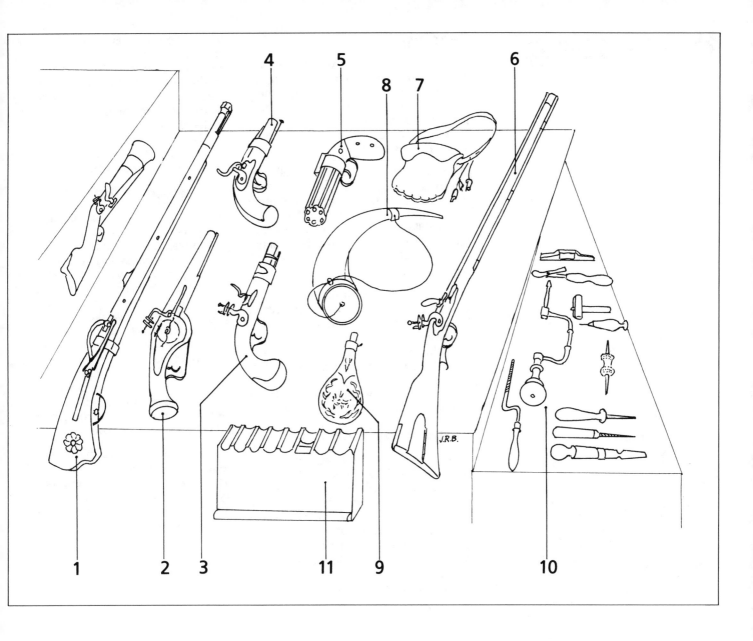

Guns, Hunting Gear, and Tools

1. The Matchlock: Invented c. 1400, this was the first practical ignition system. A piece of burning twine held in the S-shaped lever ignited the priming powder in the pan, sending a flame through the "touchhole" in the barrel to ignite the black powder inside.

2. The Wheellock: Invented c. 1500, this was the first ignition system to strike fire by mechanical means. A key-wound, rough-edged wheel turned against a piece of iron pyrite, creating sparks which touched off the priming powder in the pan.

3. The Flintlock: Perfected in France by 1630 and used until the 1840's. When the trigger was pulled, the flint snapped against the "frizzen," sending sparks into the firing pan.

4. The Percussion Gun: The percussion cap was patented in America in 1823. From then on nearly all new guns would have the percussion ignition system, and thousands of old flintlocks would be converted to it.

5. The Pepperbox: These multi-barreled guns found favor in the 17th century. They were a great step towards revolving-cylinder pistols.

6. American Long Rifle: Commonly known as the Kentucky or Pennsylvania Rifle, this gun evolved in the early 1700's in the eastern part of Pennsylvania. It was the most accurate rifle that had ever been made, and its manufacture was an art form.

7. Hunting Bag: The woodsman's invaluable leather bag was used to carry flints, rifle patches, bullets, a few small tools, a whetstone, a fish line and hooks, and anything else needed for wilderness survival.

8. Powder Horn: Steer, cow, and ox horns were used to carry gunpowder. Many were fashioned by hand, but there were also shops which specialized in their manufacture.

9. Powder Flask: Commercially-made flasks of brass and copper had replaced horns by the third quarter of the 19th century.

10. The Gunsmith's Tools: All kinds of metal and woodworking hand tools were used to fabricate barrels and lockplates and to make gun stocks. A few gunsmithing tools were very specialized, like the long-handled borers, reamers, and cutting tools used to finish and "rifle" barrels by cutting grooves inside them.

11. Barrel Anvil: A special anvil with furrows in it for maintaining the shape of gun barrels as they were forged ("hammer-welded") by the gunsmith.

Harvesting

Reaping

Harvest is the season in which crops are cut, carried to the barn or stackyard, and stored away. The actual cutting of the crops is known as reaping. Before the introduction of machinery in the mid-19th century, crops were reaped with the sickle and the scythe.

The sickle is the most ancient of all reaping tools. During the Stone Age, sickles were fashioned from hardwood slightly curved and edged with sharp flints. By the Middle Ages, the curved iron sickle had evolved, and remained the tool universally used until replaced by the cradle scythe in the late 18th century.

Laborers called harvest-men were hired to reap crops. Women were most often hired as "gatherers," following behind the reapers, laying the cut grain onto straw bands and tying it into bundles called sheaves. The sheaves remained in the field until the crop was dry (three days or more), then they were hauled to the barn or stackyard for threshing.

Crops of Early America

Wheat, rye, barley, and oats were the cereal grains of Europe at the time America was discovered. All four were of Old World origin and were so universal in the European farm economy that the seeds were brought along on most colonizing ventures to America. Four other plants had an important place in pioneer agriculture: peas, buckwheat, corn (maize), and hay. Peas and buckwheat were brought from Europe and corn was introduced to the settlers by the Native Americans. Although there were native grasses (such as the famous Kentucky Bluegrass), they produced only a scanty hay crop. As large amounts of hay were needed to provide for the winter feeding of farm animals, it was necessary to plant hay and the early settlers imported red clover and timothy from Europe.

Harvesting in America

By the end of the 18th century, the cradle scythe had been invented and was a great advance over the sickle for speed and efficiency in reaping grain crops. It was adopted wherever grain was grown in America. "Cradling" was a community job. A number of men (hired hands, neighbors, migrant workers) worked in rows across a field, swinging their "cradles" rhythmically. On the average, one man could reap about 2½ acres of grain in a day. Hay was reaped (mown) with the mowing scythe in the same manner that it had been harvested in Europe for centuries. An acre of hay could be cut in a day by an expert mower.

As reaping and mowing machinery began to replace the old hand tools towards the end of the 19th century, scythes were relegated to odd jobs about the farm such as cutting down nettles and weeds.

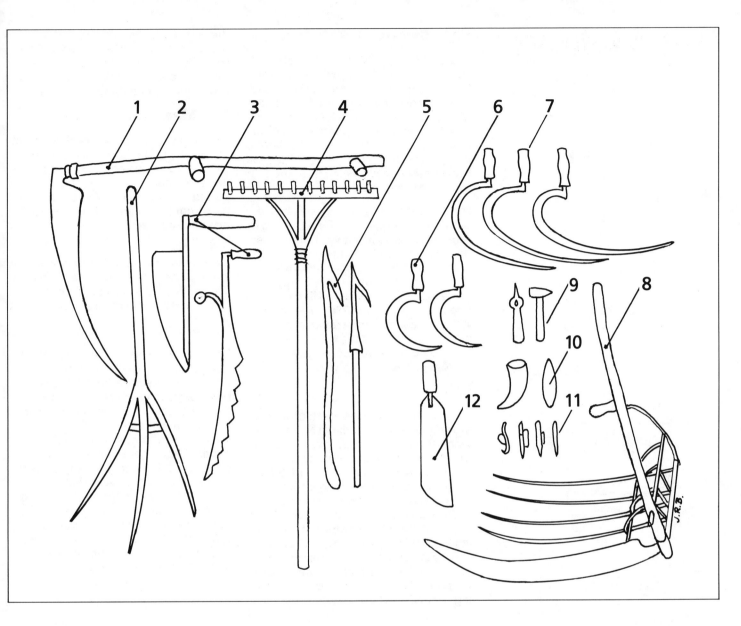

Harvesting Tools

1. Mowing Scythe:	Used mainly for cutting hay. The length and shape of the handle varied to suit individual and regional preferences.		**8. Cradle Scythe:**	A mowing scythe with several long wooden "fingers." The function of this apparatus was to catch and hold the grain after the blade cut it; then, by a slight tip of the "cradle," it slid off to lie in a neat row (swath).
2. Hay Fork:	Used to toss dry hay on and off the wagon, to build haystacks, or to toss hay into the barn loft.		**9. Scythe Hammer & Anvil:**	The pointed anvil was driven into a log and a dull scythe blade was placed on its wedge top to be straightened and sharpened by tapping along the cutting edge with the hammer.
3. Hay Knives:	Used to cut blocks of hay from the stack, which became very dense and compact after a short time. Two 19th-century types are shown.			
4. Hay Rake:	Used to turn cut hay in the field, to hasten drying.		**10. Mower's Horn & Whetstone:**	The whetstone was used to hone the scythe blade after sharpening. When not in use, it hung from the scytheman's belt in a cow's horn with a hook attached. Mower's horns were often ornamented with notches, designs, and initials.
5. Hay Hooks:	Used in handling loose hay for feeding livestock. It was stuck into the stack and twisted so that the barb became entwined with the hay.			
6. Sickles:	Universal and ancient tool for reaping grain crops. Sharp fine teeth were cut on the inside edge of the curved blade.		**11. Husking Pegs:**	Pegs of metal, ivory, bone, or wood used to aid in stripping away the husks of corn, and to loosen kernels prior to shelling.
7. Reaping Hook:	Similar to the sickle, but having no teeth.		**12. Corn Knife:**	Machete-like knife used to cut corn. Its heavy blade was capable of slashing through three or four stalks in one blow.

Hat Making

Hats Throughout History

Head coverings of skin, cloth, leather, and felt have been worn since ancient times. Until the 14th century, the universal head covering was some form of the simple, close-fitting cap. By the 16th century, the beret had appeared. It was this little hat, with its low crown and narrow brim, that was the forerunner of the tall beaver hats prized by men from the 17th to the 19th centuries.

For the first two hundred years, broad-brimmed hats dominated men's styles in America. Besides being worn for protection, hats served to designate social class and political and religious affiliations. During the 18th century, the "three-cornered" hat known as the Tricorne was popular. From about 1790 through the 19th century, the high-crowned beaver hat with narrow rolling brim (the "stovepipe" hat) was worn by well-dressed gentlemen everywhere.

Felt

Felt is a dense, compact cloth produced by matting together animal fibers (fur or wool) through a process involving heat, friction, and moisture. Since ancient times, felt has been a favored material for hats because it is stronger than woven material, will not ravel or tear easily, and is more water resistant than fabric. By the 15th century, felt hat making was an important trade in Europe. The most desirable fur for felt hats was beaver. Due to the great vogue for beaver hats, that animal's European breeding grounds had been so depleted by the end of the 16th century that another source of beaver fur was needed. The New World supplied this source, and the fur trade became a primary factor in the exploration and settling of America.

Hat Making in America

Felt hat making was one of the earliest and most profitable colonial industries. By 1730, so many hats were being manufactured and exported that the British passed a law prohibiting the export of hats from the colonies. This "Hat Act" was ignored, and the industry continued to thrive.

By 1810, the annual value of hats made in the United States was near 10 million dollars. By 1850, over 14 million dollars worth of hats were manufactured yearly.

Hatboxes

Since hats were valued and kept from one generation to the next (they were often left as bequests in wills), colorful boxes were made to carry and store them. Hatboxes were sometimes made of wood and leather, but the majority were made of pasteboard (layers of paper glued together) covered with wallpaper printed in gay designs. Used by men and women alike, hatboxes were most popular during the second quarter of the 19th century. Those that survive represent a unique and individual phase of American pictorial art and preserve some of the earliest color printing done in America.

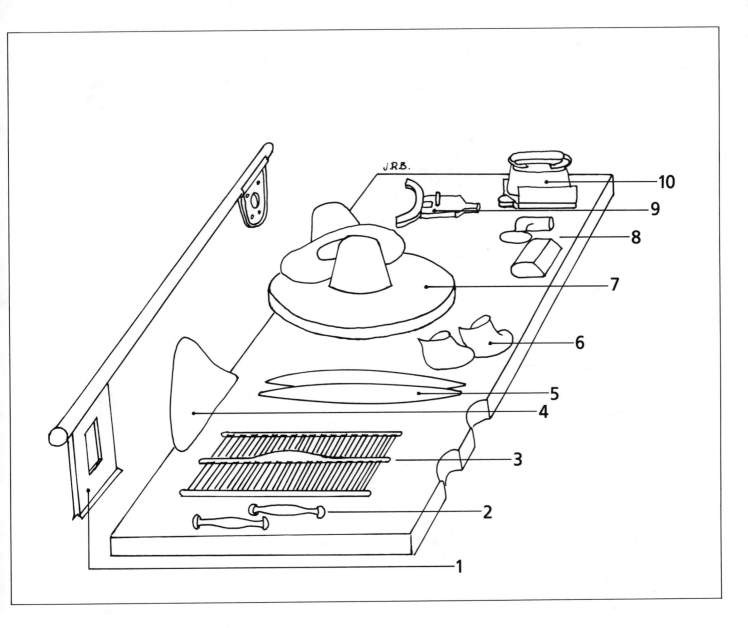

J.R.B.

Hat Making Tools

1. Hatter's Bow: Hung from the ceiling above a mass of fur fibers on the work bench. The cat-gut string was plucked and set to vibrating amongst the fibers, causing them to interlace and produce a semi-compact, oval sheet of fibers called a "batt."

2. Bow Pins: Used to pluck the string of a bow.

3. Hatter's Basket: Used to press and rub a batt of fur fibers covered with leather, to begin the felting process.

4. Hood: Two batts joined together and worked by hand into a flat, conical shape; also called a "hat body."

5. Hatter's Pins: In a process called "planking," the hood was boiled in a large open kettle of water, manipulated by hand, and rolled with these pins. This took several hours, and caused the hood to shrink and become much thicker.

6. Hatter's Gloves: Worn to protect the hatter's hands during the planking process.

7. Hatter's Block & Rimboard: Crown-shaped wooden block mounted on a board over which the felted hood was placed and worked into place (called blocking the hat).

8. Tollickers: Blocks of hardwood used in the blocking process to flatten, smooth, and work excess moisture from the hat.

9. Rimjack: Tool with an adjustable blade used to cut the rim of the hat to any desired size and shape.

10. Hatter's Goose: Iron used to press the hat so that the nap would lie in one direction and be smooth and shiny. Heated with a red-hot "slug" placed in its hollow core.

Healing Arts

The tools used for the healing arts reflect the profound changes that took place in the medical professions in America during the eighteenth and nineteenth centuries.

Before the nineteenth century, doctors, surgeons, apothecaries, and physicians employed medical techniques that had been in use for centuries. Illness was seen as physical imbalance. Treatment was supposed to restore the balance—usually by eliminating the symptoms of disease. Doctors let blood to reduce fevers or drew "poisons" to the surface with vacuum cups. Herbs were prescribed to relieve symptoms. Surgical tools resembled the tools of the butcher.

In the nineteenth century, the invention of the microscope, the discovery of bacteria, and the systematic study of disease brought a new perspective to the healing arts. Doctors were trained to study the symptoms of disease, not simply eliminate them. Understanding the cause of illness helped the trained physician to treat the disease, not the symptom. Diagnosis became as important as treatment, and the tools of the physician reflected that change. Stethoscopes for listening, specula for looking, and a variety of probes and examining tools for exploring became the basic tools of the physician. Surgical tools were specialized and finely made, and tools such as inoculating sets were developed to treat the newly discovered causes of disease.

Home Remedies

People have always used things like "magical" healing stones, patented medicine, and even chicken soup to take care of themselves at home. Even in societies with "medicine men" or doctors, health care is primarily a matter of using home remedies passed along as popular wisdom.

Some home remedies relied on the healing powers of certain herbs, chemical powders, and potions. Some of these treatments were effective and continue to be used. Many of them, however, had little real value for curing disease.

In the nineteenth century, the availability of new materials changed the tools associated with home remedies. Glass, tin, brass, and pewter replaced wood as the primary material. Herbs and minerals used for medicinal purposes for centuries were distilled and refined using the chemical methods developed during the nineteenth century.

Hearing Aids

Horn and tortoise shell transmit sound more effectively than less flexible materials, so they were used to aid hearing. Ear

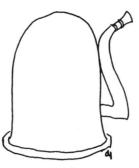

Ear Trumpet

Glasses

trumpets were among the first objects to utilize rubber and plastic as those materials became available.

Visual Aids

The ophthalmoscope used for observing the focus of a patient's eye was not invented until the mid 1850's. Before that, however, people had discovered that lenses of various strengths could aid eyesight, and corrective glasses appeared in the Colonies in the eighteenth century.

Benjamin Franklin is credited with the idea of bi-focals—glasses for improving the focus of things far away as well as nearby.

Feeding Aids

The availability of such materials as glass and tin at the end of the eighteenth and beginning of the nineteenth century made bottle-feeding of infants possible. Many of these feeders were used for invalids as well as infants.

The Apothecary

Before the period of scientific medicine, herbs and chemical compounds were used to treat the symptoms of disease. The art of the apothecary can be traced back to ancient times, and apothecary scales, the mortar and pestle for grinding medicines, and the pill machine have changed little over the centuries.

Early Americans frequently turned to the pharmacist as the primary source of health care in their communities. He could recommend prescriptions, perform minor operations, and serve as the community dentist.

In the nineteenth century, knowledge about the causes of disease, the properties of certain compounds, and the chemical

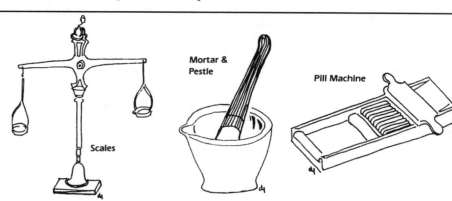

Scales

Mortar & Pestle

Pill Machine

preparation of medicines changed the role of the pharmacist in the community. The doctor diagnosed disease, and the pharmacist dispensed prescribed drugs rather than treating the patient alone.

The new interest in "scientific" cures led to another kind of product for the pharmacist—packaged "patent" medicine sold without prescriptions to those who chose not to rely on a physician's diagnosis.

The Physician

The travelling kit of the eighteenth-century physician illustrates the emphasis early medical practice placed on treating the symptoms of disease. It contained a variety of herbs and compounds, lancets for piercing veins and letting blood, and suction cups for drawing "poisons" and illness to the surface or away from affected areas. Hot glass or metal cups created a vacuum as they cooled, causing blood to rise to the surface of the skin. A skilled practitioner used the cups "dry" or lacerated the skin with a scarificator to draw fluid from the victim. The most merciful scarificators were small, spring loaded brass cubes that made a series of simultaneous cuts.

The "black bag" of the nineteenth century physician included a selection of scientifically prepared medicines and tools for examining and diagnosing patients. The first stethoscope for listening to the chest was invented about 1820, the otoscope for looking into the ears came somewhat later.

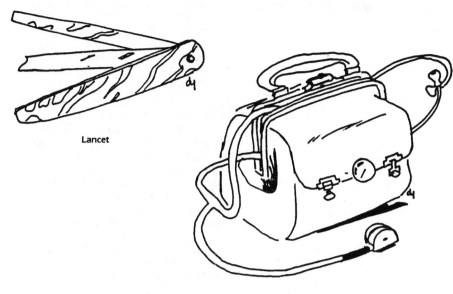

Lancet

Bag & Stethoscope

The Surgeon

Before the beginning of the nineteenth century surgeons were often associated with pharmacies. Though they performed operations, amputations and often did dental work, they did not usually have a great deal of medical training. In the age before anesthetics, surgeons required tools that enabled them to work quickly rather than carefully.

Early hospitals were not places for surgery. The Pennsylvania Hospital (founded in 1751) was the first general hospital in America. It functioned more as a care facility for the poor than a modern hospital.

As scientific medicine addressed the concerns of diagnosis and the cause of disease, medical schools were founded in association with hospitals. The hospitals became important centers for experimentation, study, and teaching. Better knowledge of the human body and more sophisticated tools enabled hospital surgeons to perform delicate operations, and hospitals became places where surgery was performed.

Diagnostic tools like microscopes eventually became common in hospitals, and when inhalers for ether were developed to anesthetize the patient, surgery developed into a very skilled art that relied on extensive medical knowledge.

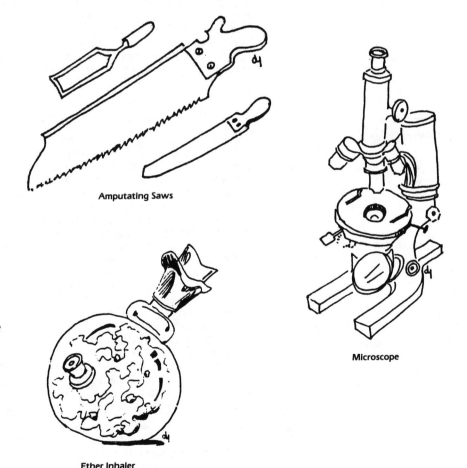

Amputating Saws

Microscope

Ether Inhaler

Hornsmithing and Shell Working

Hornsmiths fabricated combs and decorative accessories, as well as useful household items such as drinking vessels, bowls, and ladles from the horns of cattle and oxen, although buffalo, sheep, goat, or antelope horn was also used. The ready availability of horn and its unique, plastic properties made it an important material in early America. One of the earliest recorded hornsmiths, Enoch Noyes of West Newbury, Massachusetts, had established a business by 1759.

Noyes taught his trade to the Hill family of Leominster, Massachusetts, and by 1794 the Hills employed 20 workmen in their comb "factory." Later, Leominster became the center of the comb industry in America, producing products worth $250,000 in 1873. Horn products were also made in Binghamton, New York, Newark, New Jersey, and Philadelphia, Pennsylvania. The industry flourished until the end of the 19th century, when the practice of dehorning cattle decreased the supply of raw materials and celluloid was developed as a substitute for horn.

Horn is composed of substantial quantities of gelatin, which makes it an easy material to cut, bend, and mold when it is softened by heat. First, the horn was removed from the animal, and the hornsmith sawed off both ends of the horn. Then, after soaking the horn for several days, he boiled it in water or oil, using a large pot and long handled tongs. When

the horn was soft, he slit it from end to end and flattened it between heated iron plates to which pressure was applied. A flat "plate" was obtained in this way, and the plate of horn was ready to be cut into combs.

Most of the tools in the Museum collection were used by the Crouse family who came from Germany before the Revolution and settled in Lancaster County, Pennsylvania. For four generations, this family made horn combs, first with hand tools, and after 1900, with steam driven machinery.

In the early 19th century, several machines were developed to improve the quality of horn combs and the rapidity with which they could be made. The horn splitting machine utilized an adjustable horizontal blade that could shave the rough outer surface of the horn and also cut it to any thickness. The twinning machine was invented by David Noyes in 1817. It utilized a vertical blade that made it possible to cut two combs at once out of a single blank (the teeth in one comb were the gaps in the other one). Other developments included the circular saw, another machine for cutting teeth. Machines such as these enabled a relatively small number of establishments to meet the nation's great demand for hair combs. In 1850, there were 151 manufacturers of hair combs in the United States employing approximately 1800 people.

Shell Working

Tortoise shell has long been admired as one of the most decorative of all natural materials. It was used by the Greeks and Romans as an inlay material to decorate furniture and the doors and pillars of houses. In America, the shell of the tropical hawksbill tortoise which was imported from the Caribbean was used to produce combs and a wide variety of personal and household articles. The process of preparing and using tortoise shell was slow and difficult, and it required a great deal of skill. In the hands of an experienced craftsman, tortoise shell was an extremely pliable and versatile material: it could be carved, welded, sawn, softened, and twisted into many shapes. Large objects had to be made from several layers of shell welded together. Scraps of the valuable material were utilized for small ornaments.

Tortoise shell combs were among the prized possessions of an 18th century family, and they were often passed from one generation to the next. It was not until the 19th century that tortoise objects were produced in America in large quantities. Tortoise shell hair ornaments, combs, fans, and jewelry (lockets, pendants, brooches, and earrings) were highly

fashionable in America from 1860-1885. Perhaps the most prolific period for the use of this material was from 1890 to 1915. It was used for everything from the traditional "back," "puff," and "side" combs to hair pins, dressing table sets, boxes for cigarettes, matches, and calling cards, hatpins, fans, eyeglasses, needlework tools, and pocket knife handles. With the development of celluloid in the late 19th century, the craft of shell working began to decline, and by the early 20th century, tortoise shell had been replaced by rubber and plastics. Its unique marking, texture, and mellow glow give it a special aesthetic quality which has scarcely been equalled by modern materials.

Most of the tortoise shell combs and objects on exhibit were made by Harry E. Davis of Philadelphia, Pennsylvania. One of the last craftsmen to work in this medium, Mr. Davis was born in Rockville, Pennsylvania in 1875. At the age of 13 he was apprenticed to a manufacturer of "tortoise shell combs and novelties" in Philadelphia. Harry Davis manufactured tortoise shell objects on Sansom Street in Philadelphia and in Providence, Rhode Island until his death in 1967.

Comb Making Tools

Standing Horse & Drawknife

A sheet of flattened horn was placed on the "horse" and held in place with the foot lever. With various heavy drawknives (shaves) the comb maker smoothed the rough horn.

Bench & Clamp

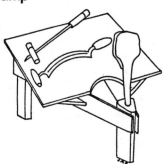

A wooden clamping vice known as a "clams" held the comb blank so that the seated comb maker could cut the blanks at eye level.

Grailles

Special comb maker's files for widening the spaces between the cut teeth and smoothing the sides of the teeth.

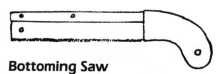

Carlet and Topper

Files for pointing and finishing the ends of hand-cut teeth and smoothing between teeth.

Quarnets

Course rasps resembling mason's trowels. The horn plate was smoothed to a uniform thickness with these.

Gauge Leaf Saw

A device with two blades, one set lower than the other, for cutting combs by hand. The lower blade cut the comb tooth while the upper one scored a notch for the next, thus assuring uniform spacing of the teeth.

Bottoming Saw

Saw with specially cut teeth used to remove excess horn from between comb teeth.

Shell Working Tools

Essentially the same skills and tools were used in working with both tortoise shell and horn. The materials themselves, though, have substantially different characteristics—tortoise is less fibrous than horn and harder and more brittle—so certain techniques of preparing and working the raw materials varied.

Drawknife

Used to shave the softened and flattened shell plates to a desired thickness.

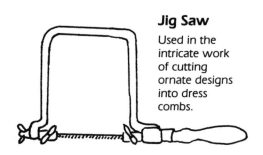

Mandrel

The curved shapes of fancy dress combs (the "back" and "side" combs highly fashionable in the 19th century) was achieved by bending the heated shell around a wooden form or "mandrel."

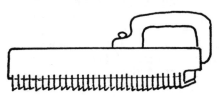

Quarnet

Rasp-like tool for final shaving and smoothing of the shell plate.

Jig Saw

Used in the intricate work of cutting ornate designs into dress combs.

Grailles

Special comb maker's files for smoothing the spaces between the cut teeth, and for smoothing their sides.

Kitchen Utensils

The Kitchen Fireside

The kitchen in the homes of our ancestors was the most cheerful and lived-in room of the house, and its heart was the fireplace. The one-room structures of the first settlers were built around a fireplace. Later dwellings had additional rooms and a second floor, but the kitchen remained the central room of the house. For over two centuries Americans depended upon the fireplace for their survival. It had many uses besides providing heat and light. All cooking was done over the fire, which was kept burning almost continuously. Cook-stoves did not become common until the mid-19th century. The fireplace served for drying clothes, herbs, and fruits and vegetables, providing coals which were used in foot and bed warmers and to light pipes, and supplying valuable ashes for use in soap and potash making.

Food Service Utensils

Throughout the colonial era and into the 19th century, food serving utensils called "treenware" were often made of wood. Wooden plates, bowls, and large serving dishes called "trenchers" were carved by farmers and coopers. Pewter articles were not uncommon in average households, but were cherished as symbols of elegance rather than used as everyday wares. Plates, bowls, and collanders were also made of earthenware "country" pottery. Horn and bone were fashioned into spoons, fork and knife handles, and drinking cups. Dippers and ladles were made of copper, brass, iron, wood, horn, and gourds.

Food in Early America

A great deal of time and effort was expended in the procurement, preservation, and preparation of food. Of the native food supplies, the three most important to the colonists were corn, fish, and game. "Indian corn" saved the first settlers' lives and, prepared in many ways, it was the mainstay of diet throughout the 17th century. The native pumpkin, or "pompion," was another valuable food. It was mashed, roasted, stewed, dried, and made into "punkin bread." By the 18th century beans, peas, squash, potatoes, parsnips, turnips, and carrots had become standard fare. Wild game and fowl, fish and shellfish, and later, domesticated pigs and cattle provided our ancestors with meat.

Cookbooks and Recipes

The present diversity of cooking and eating habits in America had its beginnings with the first settlers from Europe. Ethnic, geographical, and economic differences determined from the beginning not only what types of food the colonists would eat, but when they would eat, how much, and how their food would be prepared.

American Cookery, by Amelia Simmons, published in 1796, was the first American cookbook. After 1800 a flood of native cookbooks appeared, and it was in these books that recipes for many dishes that had been prepared for 150 years finally found their way into print. Early recipes (or "receipts") indicate that the results of early American cookery were not so very different from dishes prepared by modern cooks, despite the great difference in their manner of preparation.

To Roast Lamb: Lay it down to a good clear fire that will want little stirring; then baste it with butter, and dust on a little flour . . . a little before you take it up, baste it again . . . and sprinkle on a little salt and parsley shred fine. Send it up to table with a nice salad, mint sauce, green peas, french beans or colliflower.
The Frugal Housewife, 1772

To Make Indian Corn Pudding: Three pints scalded milk, seven spoons fine Indian meal. Stir well together while hot. Let stand till cooled; add seven eggs, half pound raisins, four ounces butter, spice, and sugar. Bake one and one half hours.
American Cookery, 1796

To Make Chouder: Take a bass weighing four pounds, boil half an hour; take six slices raw pork, fry them till the lard is nearly extracted; one dozen crackers soaked in cold water five minutes. Put the bass, pork, and crackers into the lard, and fry for twenty minutes. Serve with potatoes, pickles, apple sauce or mangoes. Garnish with green parsley.
New American Cookery, 1805

To Roast Young Chickens: When you kill young chickens, pluck them very carefully, truss and put them down to a good fire. Dredge and baste them with lard, they will take a quarter of an hour in roasting. Froth them up, lay them on a dish, put butter and parsley on them, and serve them up hot.
The Virginia Housewife, 1825

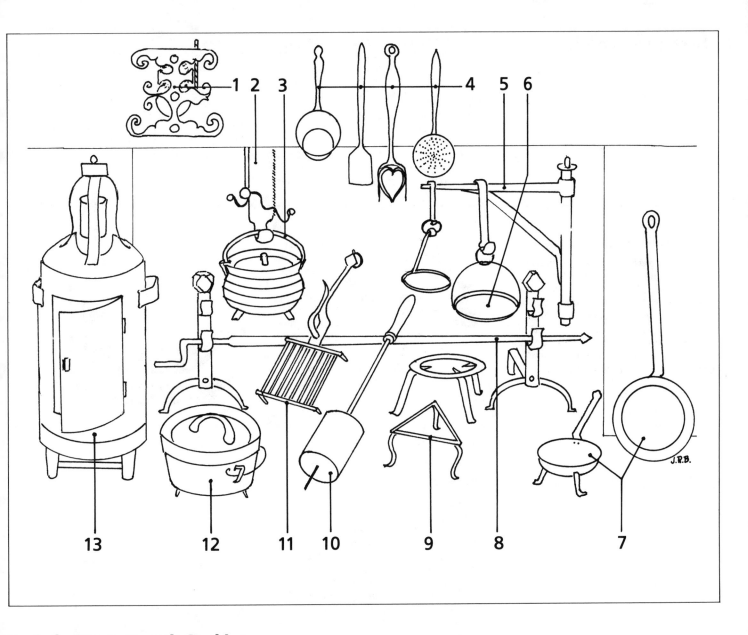

Tools for Open Hearth Cooking

1. Clock Jack: Mechanical device (run by weights and gears) for turning the long iron spit in front of the fire. A belt connected the jack and spit.

2. Trammel: Adjustable iron hook from which cooking pots, kettles, and griddles were hung over the fire. Many types, often ornate, were made by blacksmiths.

3. Iron Pot: Much of the family cooking was done in heavy iron pots. They were valued possessions and were handed down from one generation to the next.

4. Ladles, Spatulas, Forks, and Skimmers: Long-handled tools usually made of copper, iron, and brass were needed to cook and handle food over the hot coals.

5. Swinging Crane: Swinging iron bar hinged to the side wall of the fireplace which replaced the old wooden or iron "back-bar" placed above the fire inside the chimney.

6. Griddles: Flat cakes of corn, wheat, rye, oats, and buckwheat were baked on these iron plates with hooped handles.

7. Frying Pan and Skillet: Like most of the other open-fire utensils, these stood on legs and/or had long handles.

8. Andirons and Spit: A pair of andirons or "fire-dogs" was needed to hold logs and to provide a support for the long spit which was used to roast meat and fowl.

9. Trivets: 3-legged stands used to hold pots of food over the coals, on the hearth, and at the table.

10. Coffee Roaster: Coffee beans were placed inside and the roaster was turned on its point in the coals.

11. Gridiron: For broiling fish and meat in the coals.

12. Dutch Oven: Also known as "bake kettles," these were placed in the coals, and embers were heaped on the recessed lid. Used to bake bread, biscuits, and shortcake.

13. Reflecting Oven: By 1790 tin reflecting ovens or "Roasting Kitchens" were being used to roast meat. The open back faced the fire and the meat was placed on a spit inside. The spit turned by means of a hand crank or a key-wound geared device called a "meat jack."

Lighting

For thousands of years people relied on traditional, simple lighting devices to illuminate their homes and work places. All of these lighting devices worked on a single principle. They converted a fuel into a gas that would burn.

There were many drawbacks to early lighting devices. Most of them smoked, smelled bad, and dripped fuel. They needed frequent attention, and their light was only a bit brighter than candlelight. During the eighteenth century, the design of lighting devices changed rapidly because of developments in chemistry and the availability of sheet metals. New fuels that gave more brilliant light were used.

In the 1850's, the discovery of a method for refining kerosene solved the problems of convenience and safety that inventors had wrestled with for almost a century. The invention of the kerosene lamp marked the beginning of the modern era of lighting.

600 B.C.
Lamps—Oil and Grease

At a very early date people found that a shallow vessel of oil or grease with a wick laid in it could be used to provide light. As the lamp burned, the fuel, whether olive oil, fish oil, or liquid fat, was drawn to the end of the rush or twisted fiber wick by capillary action. The heat of the flame vaporized the fuel into a flammable gas.

Crusie

The crusie may have originated on the coast of Scotland or France where shell lamps were once used and fish oil was readily available as a fuel. To burn steadily, the crusie requires regular attention. the reservoir must be filled, and the wick must be adjusted. Besides needing attention, the crusie smoked and smelled bad when it burned.

Betty Lamp

The betty lamp is much like the crusie in design, but it has one important improvement. The betty has a slanting, half-round tube attached to the bottom of the pan. This tube holds the wick just inside the edge of the pan so that any grease dripping from the wick runs back into the fuel reservoir. The name of the betty lamp may come from this wick support feature, which made it a "better" lamp than its predecessor, the crusie.

Stand and Trammel

The light given by oil and grease lamps is only a little brighter than candlelight. To direct the dim light of the grease lamp to best advantage, the lamps were set on short wooden or tin stands. The stand raised the lamp so its light spread further. The base of the stand kept the lamp from dripping fuel on the table. The trammel is a saw-toothed hanging device. A lamp suspended from a trammel could be raised or lowered to a convenient height.

500 B.C.
Splints and Rushlights

Splints are long slivers of birch or resinous wood, and rushlights are pieces of meadow rush soaked in fat. Both can be burned to produce light. Like torches, splints and rushlights are consumed as they burn. The resin or fat they are saturated with makes them burn slowly and brightly.

Splints & Splint Holder

Splints could be carried about in the hand or even held in the mouth, but people also used holders to grip the splints at the proper angle for burning. Splints were cheap, but they were not as convenient as candles because they burned with a sizzling flame that produced smoke. They also dropped burning embers and dripped black pitch.

Splints were wedged in the metal tongue of the splint holder. The cone-shaped socket that is part of many splint holders was probably first made to extinguish a splint rather than to hold a candle.

Rushlight Holder

Rush is too fragile to be wedged like a splint, so rushlight holders had pivoting metal jaws to grip the pithy rush. Rushlight holders were used in England, and possibly in New England, during the same period that candles were used.

The rushlight burned more clearly than a splint although it needed the same constant attention. A rushlight two and a half feet long would burn about an hour, and it needed adjustment every ten minutes or so.

A.D. 600
Candles

Like rushlights, candles burn fat or wax and are held in a holder while they burn. A candle is made of a fiber wick, usually twisted cotton, surrounded by a solid fuel such as tallow or wax. When the wick is lit, it heats the solid fuel into a liquid that is drawn up the wick to burn as a flammable gas.

Dipped Candles

Candle tallow was made by rendering the fat of sheep or cattle. A wick could be repeatedly dipped into melted tallow and cooled until a candle was formed. A "dipping reel" made it possible to dip many candles at once. Dipped candles were usually made from poorer tallow, so they were soft and apt to bend, run, and smoke unless they were trimmed frequently.

Candle Holder

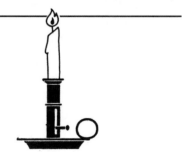

Candlesticks supplied with a handle and a drip pan for catching drips were called candle holders. Candlesticks and candle holders were improved by the addition of a push-up slide that ejected the candle stub and kept the candlelight at an even height.

Molded Candles

To make molded candles, tallow was poured into molds of tin, pewter, or earthenware that had been strung with wicks. The hardened candles could be pulled from the mold. Waxes such as beeswax or bayberry wax were added to tallow to make harder, longer burning candles.

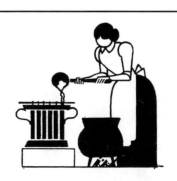

A.D. 900
Lanterns and Torches

Lanterns and torches are for use outdoors. A lantern encloses a lighting device such as a candle or an oil lamp in a portable, weatherproof container. A torch provides light by burning a large, fuel-soaked wick.

Torch

The torch is an early outdoor lighting device that burned fibers soaked in wax or resin, or bound strips of wood. The name "torch" later came to be applied to any outdoor lighting device that burned a large wick. Typical of later torches, a campaign torch is like an oil lamp mounted on a pole. Campaign torches have wicks and burn oil, but the wick is large and rope-like.

Pierced Tin Lantern

A durable, lightweight, windproof lantern could be made by enclosing a candle in a pierced tin container. The light was dim— but the pierced tin lantern could be used safely in a barn around hay and chaff.

Glass Lantern

Adding a transparent window to a lantern allowed more light to shine out. Early lanterns with windows were made out of a wood or metal frame fitted with thin sheets of cow's horn or mica.

Lights for Working

Lighting devices were often created for special purposes. The glass globed railroad lantern that burned whale oil, and later kerosene, had a bail that could be looped over a worker's arm. Its wire guards protected the glass from breaking. The little miner's lamp, shaped like a coffeepot with a large spout, was hung on the front of the miner's cap to light his way underground.

1780
Lamps—Whale Oil to Kerosene

Starting in the late 1700's, the design of lamps changed rapidly. The slanting wick support of the betty lamp was replaced by an upright, central wick tube. Fuel reservoirs were sealed to make oil-tight fonts. Better fuels such as burning fluid and kerosene were discovered that were free-flowing, clean, and highly combustible.

Whale Oil Lamp

Oil rendered from the fat of whales was a superior fuel to animal fats. It burned with less smoke and without a disagreeable smell, and it was more readily absorbed by the wick. The innovative design of whale oil lamps included a leak-proof font and one or more upright, central wicks that radiated light like a candle.

Burning Fluid Lamp

Fuel mixtures called "burning fluids" combined such ingredients as camphene (turpentine) and alcohol. Even though they were dangerous, burning fluids were popular because they flowed freely, burned without residue or odor, and gave a brilliant light. Burning fluids were abandoned in the 1860's when kerosene, a safer fuel, became widely available.

Kerosene Lamp

Kerosene was a clean, inexpensive fuel refined from petroleum. It quickly replaced other fuels. Kerosene lamps required extra air flow near the wick for greater combustion. The flat, adjustable wick was surrounded by a metal dome "deflector" that channelled air to the flame. The glass chimney became a standard feature of kerosene lamps because it protected the flame and increased the flow of air past the wick.

Lumbering

Because of the quantity of timber which the settlers encountered in the vast forests of eastern North America, lumber became one of the colonies' first and most profitable exported products. The great demand for lumber was a primary factor in the expansion of the seaboard settlements towards the interior of the country. The lumberer's business consisted of cutting trees down in the forest, then hauling or floating them down streams to sawmills where they were cut into boards, planks, joists, etc. Since wood products were one of the first needs of a community, water-powered sawmills were erected everywhere as settlement expanded. Sawmills were built as early as 1620.

The Domestic Need

Building America required wood to make houses, tools, bridges, furniture, and utensils. Wood was the raw material for many trades such as coopering, wheelwrighting, and shingle making. Great quantities of wood were needed as a source for charcoal, tar, turpentine, and potash. Wood was used in so many ways that the 18th century has been called "America's Wooden Age."

The Demand From Abroad

England and the West Indies provided a ready market for boards, barrel staves, shingles, and ships' masts and spars. In 1671, New Hampshire alone sent 20,000 tons of boards and barrel staves and ten ships "laden with masts" abroad. In the three-year period from 1771-1773 almost 77 million feet of boards were shipped from the colonies to the West Indies.

The 19th Century

In 1850 only the cotton and flour industries surpassed lumbering in the annual value of their products. In 1859 America produced almost 94 million dollars worth of lumber.

Until about 1830 Maine was the center of the lumber industry, but the rapid depletion of the eastern forests caused the industry to shift towards the midwestern states. This westward movement continued throughout the 19th century, and by the 20th century the Northwest had become the logging center of the country.

River Rafting

Large scale milling was often carried out at sawmills located in commercial centers. By connecting logs together, great rafts were made of timber cut in the mountains. The rafts were floated down rivers and canals to commercial mills. Rafting began about 1650 and continued until the end of the 19th century.

Rafting in Pennsylvania reached its peak in the decade from 1875 to 1885. In the "boom year" of 1875, over 3000 rafts passed down the Delaware River. The largest on record was 215 feet long and contained 120,000 feet of lumber.

The depletion of timber in the river valleys and the establishment of a railroad network throughout the country brought river rafting to an end.

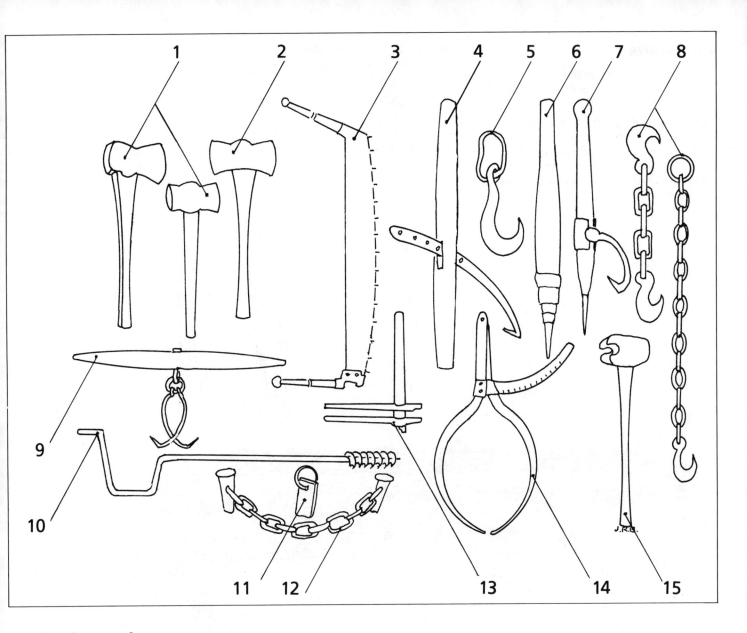

Lumbering Tools

1. Felling Axe:	Master tool of the logging industry. Used for felling trees and cutting off and chopping up limbs.
2. Double-Bitted Axe:	Axe with two bits (cutting edges). This tool appeared in Maine and Pennsylvania around 1850 and largely replaced the felling axe, as it gave twice the service between sharpening.
3. Cross-Cut Saw:	Two-man saw which began to replace axes around 1880, when improvements in teeth and methods of sharpening and tempering steel allowed for the production of saws that could fell timber faster than axes.
4. Cant Hook:	Tool for rolling logs. The spur (curved iron hook at lower end) and staff formed "jaws" with which a log could be grasped and rolled by applying leverage.
5. Ring Dog:	Alternative to the cant hook. A staff or crow bar was thrust through the ring and leverage was applied.
6. Jam Pike:	Used to shift the position of logs and to pry free logs which became "jammed up" during their transport down mountain streams to the sawmill.

7. Peavey:	Combination cant hook and jam pike invented by a New York blacksmith named John Peavey in 1870. It both rolled and pried and quickly became a standard logging tool.
8. Log Grabs and Chains:	Used to drag logs, attach them to each other, and to secure logs to transport vehicles such as sleds and wagons.
9. Log Tongs:	Four men, using two of these, could carry a large log.
10. Raft Auger:	Used to drill holes in logs in order to attach them to each other with saplings and wooden pegs.
11. Snub Ring:	Multi-purpose tool used to drag logs out of the woods, to attach them to each other, and to moor logs to the shore.
12. Raft Shackle:	Used to attach (shackle) logs to each other.
13. Sliding Scale:	Measuring tool used to find the diameter of trees and logs.
14. Calipers:	Another tool for measuring diameter.
15. Marking Axe:	Used to stamp owners' marks into the end of logs.

Log Sleds

Log sleds were used in the winter to haul logs over the snow from the forest to the sawmill.

Usually homemade, these massive wooden sleds were sometimes used singly but were more often hitched together in pairs. A pair of these ox- or horse-drawn sleds could easily carry logs over the winter snow.

Used extensively in the lumbering business until about 1880, Log Sleds (which of course could only be used in winter) were gradually replaced by tractors. The so-called "Bob Sled", which had iron-shod runners, was still being used, however, at some lumber yards and sawmills in Pennsylvania until as recently as 1925.

Log Wheels

Pulled by two horses, Log Wheels were used to transport logs from the river to a nearby sawmill.

They were backed into the water over a floating log. The log was chained to the forks of the heavy iron turn screw that ran down through the axle. As the turn screw was cranked, it lifted the forward end of the log, so that the horses could pull the wheels and the log, with its rear end dragging, up the bank to the sawmill. The very long tongue was necessary to prevent the long log from hitting the horses as they pulled the wheels.

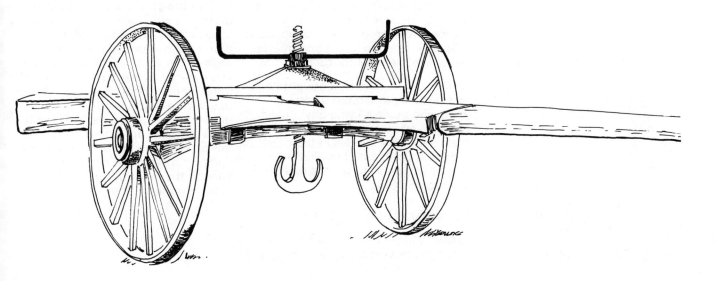

Meat Preservation

Butchering in Early America

In the 18th and 19th centuries, butchering was an important annual event on farms and homesteads throughout America. It usually took place during the warmer part of the winter when the temperature was between 34 and 40°F. Most farmers, with the help of sons, neighbors, or hired hands, did their own butchering.

Unless a farmer did custom or large-scale butchering on a regular basis, the butcher house or area was not usually a self-contained building. Slaughtering cattle, oxen, or pigs was most often done beneath the forebay of the barn, in front of or within the wagon shed, or in some other protected area.

After the animals had been slaughtered and the carcasses cut up into portions, the meat was carried to the springhouse, cellar, or kitchen to be cut into smaller pieces and prepared for curing.

In urban areas, butchers bought hogs and cattle from farmers or drovers (men who made a living buying and selling livestock), and slaughtered them in butcher houses in the city. They sold the meat at market or employed "runners" to sell the meat from door to door.

Preservation of Meat

Before refrigeration, meat had to be cured (preserved) to prevent decay and provide a year-round supply. Meat was cured in several ways.

1. Salting: Two methods of salt-curing were used: the dry-cure, in which meat was packed in salt; and the brine-cure, in which meat was immersed in a solution of salt and water.

2. Potting: This method was used when salt was in short supply. The meat was first cooked, then placed in a crock and covered with a deep layer of melted fat or lard. Meat preserved in this manner was often used on long ship voyages.

3. Drying: The settlers learned to dry meat from the Indians. The meat was cut into thin strips and dried in the sun or hung near the fire. This produced a tough, dry meat, called jerk or jerky.

4. Smoking: Also learned from the Indians, this was the method most widely used in the 19th century. More pork than beef was smoked. Pork in the form of bacon, scrapple, and sausage was a staple food in early America. The usual method of preserving pork was to salt-cure it and hang it in the smokehouse. The smoke from the fire (usually of hickory wood) completed this process, and imparted a fine, distinctive flavor to the meat. It was then hung in the cellar or springhouse and used throughout the year.

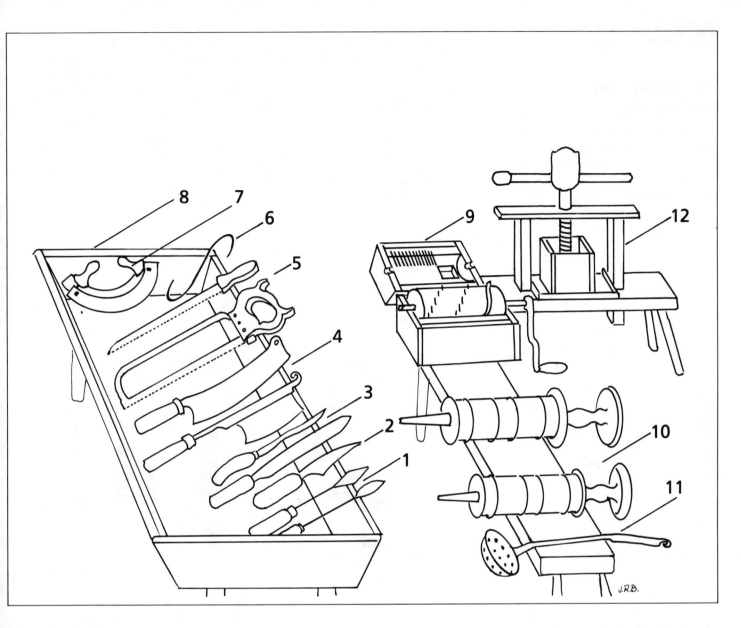

Butchering Tools

1. Hog-Sticking Knives:	The butcher killed the pig by plunging this sharp-pointed implement into its jugular vein.	**8. Chopping Bench:**	Table on which large pieces of meat were placed for cutting.
2. Hog Scrapers:	Used to remove the bristles from the pig's body, after the carcass had been scalded.	**9. Meat Grinder:**	Hand-cranked machine used to grind meat for making sausage and scrapple.
3. Butcher Knives:	Used for final shaving of the carcass before it was hung to be disemboweled.	**10. Sausage Stuffers:**	Used to make sausage. The sausage casing was fitted over the funnel-shaped outlet and a plunger forced the meat into the casing.
4. & 5. Cleavers and Saws:	Used to cut the carcass into large portions, which were then hung to cool for about 24 hours before the curing process could begin.	**11. Straining Ladle:**	Used to strain solid bits, called "cracklings," from melted fat in the process of making lard.
6. Meat Hook:	Used to hang meat from wall hooks and rafters.	**12. Lard Press:**	Used to squeeze liquid lard from the cracklings. There were many types of lard presses; this one is similar to a large sausage stuffer.
7. Meat Cutter:	Double-bladed tool used to cut large sections of meat into smaller pieces.		

Milling

Pounding and Grinding Mills

Two methods of reducing grain and corn into flour and meal have been used since prehistoric times: pounding and grinding.

Prior to the establishment of a local grist mill, and everywhere on the frontier, settlers were compelled to make do with crude hand-operated devices such as you see here, to pound and grind their grain and corn.

Pounding or **"Plumping" Mills** represent the ingenious application of water power to a wooden mortar and pestle.

Rice Querns were used to hull (shell) rice. Wooden "millstones" were used in rice querns, becaues rice is more delicate than grain or corn.

Rotary Querns (also known as hand mills) were the ancient prototypes of grist mills. The grain or corn was poured through the hole in the upper stone and ground between the revolving upper stone and the stationary lower stone. The flour meal was then discharged through the chute into a container on the ground. Simple querns like the ones on the floor represent the first use of millstones in this country; later the stones were set in wooden frames for convenience.

Rotary Querns

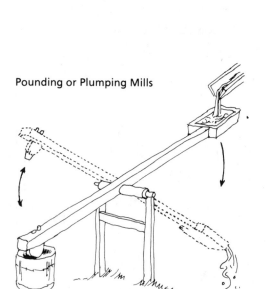

Pounding or Plumping Mills

Rice Querns

Up and Down Sawmill

This type of water-operated sawmill derives its name from the up and down motion of the saw blade.

It was powered by a crank mounted on the end of the horizontal axle of a water wheel. The log to be sawn was rolled onto the carriage, which moved forward by means of a ratchet wheel that also reversed the motion once the cut had been made. The up and down sawmill was inexpensive to build and operate and was much more efficient than hand sawing. In 1750 it was reported that a man and a boy could saw 4000 feet of one-inch pine boards in ten hours, ten times as much as could be done by hand in the same time.

The great demand for boards, planks, and rafters in America was largely supplied by this type of sawmill from 1630 until about 1840, when circular and band saws came into general use.

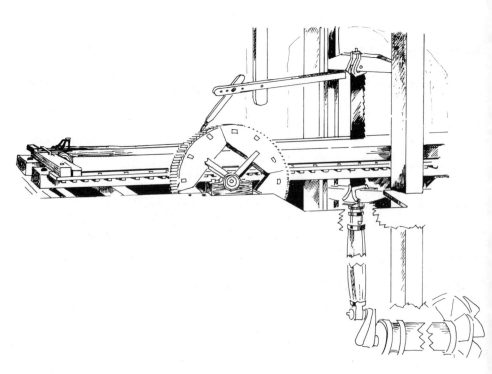

Norse Mill

The Norse Mill, also known as a Tub Mill, is a primitive and ancient type of water-powered grist mill that was used to grind corn and grain into meal and flour.

This mill was used on the sloping bank of a mountain stream for nearly a hundred years, grinding corn for "moonshine" whiskey and food. The Norse Mill differed from the common grist mill in that the water wheel was horizontal rather than vertical and was connected directly to the millstones by a shaft. This eliminated the need for a complicated gearing mechanism, making the Norse Mill the simplest and least expensive of all mills to build and operate.

Known to have been used for centuries in Europe, Turkey, and China, this type of mill was brought to Pennsylvania by Swedish immigrants in the 17th century. Scotch-Irish and French settlers introduced it to the southern states in the 18th century.

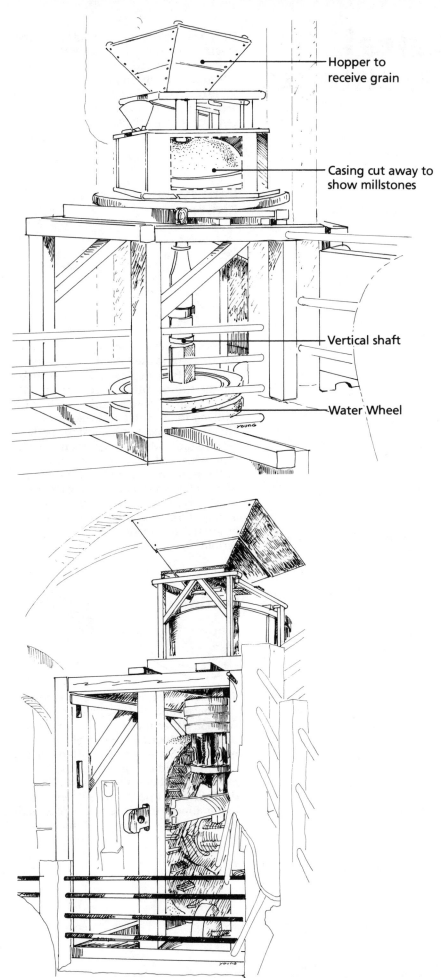

Hopper to receive grain

Casing cut away to show millstones

Vertical shaft

Water Wheel

Grist Mill

Water-powered grist mills were used to grind large quantities of cereal grain into flour.

Power from the water wheel was transmitted to the mill machinery by means of a wooden gearing system. Farmers brought their grain to the mill once or twice a week, in sacks. The sacks were hoisted to the top floor and emptied into the hopper. The grain fell through a hole in the revolving upper millstone and was ground between it and the stationary lower stone. Grooves in the stones allowed the flour to move out to the edges and into the box built around the stones. The flour was then moved along a wooden pipe to the bolter (hanging above this mill), a device for separating the flour into different grades. The farmer picked up his flour on his next trip to the mill. The miller was often paid for his work by keeping a certain amount of the flour for his own use.

Mills had to be built near running water, and roads and bridges were built to them. They became centers of trade and commerce, and towns grew up around them. This typical water-powered grist mill was assembled using parts from four different 19th century southeastern Pennsylvania mills.

Musical Instruments

Early Americans produced, adapted, and invented a variety of musical instruments to meet their needs for recreation and self-expression through music. Today, some of these instruments are considered archaic; some of them are almost forgotten. Others are still played and enjoyed just as they were hundreds of years ago.

Pennsylvania German Zithers

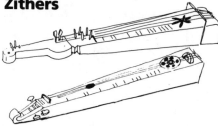

Known as "zitters" among the people who made and used them, these stringed instruments were played by either striking the strings with a "plectrum" (pick) made from a goose or turkey quill or by stroking them with a bow, like a violin. They were either held against the body or set on a table while being played. There is little evidence to document the existence of this instrument until the 16th century when it became a popular folk instrument in central and northern Europe. It is conjectured that the Mennonites brought it to America, but this is not certain.

Dulcimore

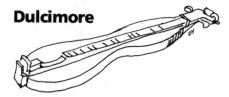

The "dulcimore" is closely related to and possibly a variant of the Pennsylvania German zither. It was peculiar to the Appalachian Mountain region of the eastern United States, and was often called a "mountain zither." In general use by mountain folk only since about 1900, the dulcimore is a true folk instrument in that its manufacture and method of play were learned strictly through oral tradition.

Hammer Dulcimer

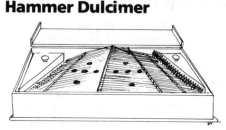

This stringed instrument may have originated in Persia as early as the 14th century. It probably evolved from the ancient psaltery. The main difference between the two is in the method of play. The strings of the psaltery were plucked; the hammer dulcimer's strings were set to vibrating by two "beaters" or hammers. The strings were stretched alternately over bridges set on the right and left sides of the trapezoidal sound box. When the leather-headed hammers struck the strings, a rich, shimmering sound was produced.

Banjos

Old documents allude to the use of a simple banjo-like instrument by the Negroes of Jamaica during the late 17th century, strongly indicating that the banjo had its roots in Africa. It became popular among American Blacks in the 18th century, and by the early 19th century its popularity had spread among the white population. The banjo appealed to the home musician and was a favorite instrument of professionals such as traveling minstrels and music hall performers.

Hurdy-Gurdy

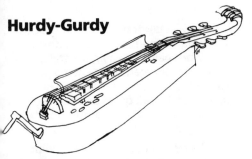

The hurdy-gurdy was basically a mechanical violin (unlike the much later "barrel organ" often referred to by the same name, which was a large music box). It was probably the earliest stringed instrument with keys. A wooden wheel turned by a hand crank caused the strings to vibrate. The vibrating length of the "tune string" was changed for each note by pressing keys; the "drone strings" pulsated continuously.

The hurdy-gurdy, used in Europe since the 10th century, embodied the spirit of early medieval music—the melody was never free from the instrument's other "voices." The instrument's popularity declined as the nature of music began to change around 1300. The new spirit emphasized harmonics and complex relationships between instruments, and the unvarying sound of drone strings did not suit this new style.

Solophone

This little stringed and keyed instrument was invented in the late 19th century in Germany and was introduced into the U.S. in 1893. In tone and manner of play it was similar to a violin, although it was laid flat on a table while being played. Wire strings were stretched across a fretboard, and above the strings was a keyboard with push-button keys which served the same purpose as a violinist's fingers. The exposed portion of the strings was bowed as the keys were pressed down.

Autoharp

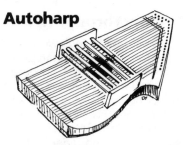

This stringed instrument appeared in America during the last quarter of the 19th century. It has 23 strings which are divided into octaves and stretched across the shallow sound box. It was commonly played by pressing down one of the bars ("mutes") and running the thumb of the right hand (equipped with a pick) across the strings to produce a chord, while the melody was picked out with the index finger.

Accordion

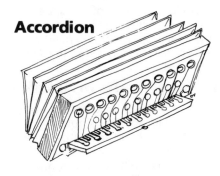

The accordion, invented in 1822, is actually a small portable organ sounded by free reeds. A free reed is a metal "tongue" extending over an aperture in the frame of the instrument. Air passing over the reed caused it to vibrate. Keys controlled the air flow, which was supplied by a hand-operated bellows. Often reeds were grouped in pairs so that each key could control two notes—one with the inflation and one with the deflation of the bellows.

Pianoforte

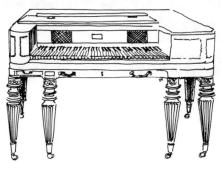

The pianoforte (today's piano) is a keyboard instrument in which hammers strike strings, causing them to sound. It was invented in 1720 by an Italian named Bartolomeo Cristofori, curator of muscial instruments at the Medici court. The name pianoforte is an Italian word meaning "soft-loud," which refers to the fact that, unlike its predecessors the harpsichord and the spinet, the tones it produced could be made louder or softer by varying the finger pressure on the keys.

This type of pianoforte was called a square piano. Unlike upright and grand pianos, its strings were parallel to the width of the piano. Square pianos were first built in 18th century Germany. The first American pianos were built in Philadelphia and Boston in the 1770's, and square pianos were among the first made. They were very popular and considerably cheaper to manufacture than the larger upright and grand pianos.

Needlework and Laundering

Needlework Through History

There are two kinds of needlework: plain needlework for purely utilitarian purposes; and "art needlework" for decorative purposes. The needle is one of man's oldest tools, and by the time the great civilizations of antiquity were flourishing, highly decorative forms of needlework were being used to embroider fabrics. Although men have practiced certain forms of needlework, this area of the decorative arts has largely been the province of women through the ages.

Tapestries, embroideries, bed furnishings, samplers, and the other products of stitchery are a unique record of history and cultural traditions, and they reflect the experience and spirit of women in nearly every part of the world. In the Old World, there were two basic kinds of needlework: the gay, naive patterns worked by peasant women, and the rich, formal designs worked by ladies of the upper classes and nobility. The influence of European (particularly English) needlework was of course strongly felt in the American colonies.

The Needlecrafts in America

Women of America documented every phase of their experience from young girlhood through old age with needlework of dignity, beauty, and originality. Their samplers, quilts, coverlets, and pictorial embroideries provide us with a unique insight into their lives and are a valuable contribution to our knowledge of the history and growth of American society.

An artistic flair and urge to decorate became evident even as colonial women undertook the colossal job of making clothes and bed covers, curtains and rugs, to keep their families and homes warm. Embroidery and appliqué designs were worked over the seams of linens, and clothing was decorated with fancy stitches to hide worn areas. As cloth items became worn beyond repair, the still usable parts were salvaged to be used again. Two very fine forms of American needlework—patchwork quilts and hooked rugs—grew directly out of this tradition of saving every precious bit of fabric.

Most forms of needlework—mending, sewing new garments, knitting and crocheting, quilting, rug-making, and even embroidery and needlepoint—were known as "busywork." Besides being the simple act of always keeping one's hands busy, busywork was a quiet respite from hard labor and a way for women to beautify and enhance their often drab environments with their own creations.

Washing and Ironing

Until the advent of modern washing machines and irons, the weekly process of washing and ironing the family's clothes was an arduous chore. Washing was done in wooden tubs, with wash and rinse water heated in big kettles over the kitchen fire or outside. Substances such as lye, potash, and carbonate of soda were used to soften water; "bluing" made of indigo dye was added to make clothes look whiter; soap was homemade from ashes and animal fat; and if starch was desired, it might be homemade from wheat.

Techniques of ironing were not so very different in early America than they are today, but the process was far more laborious and time-consuming. The old flat-irons (or sadirons) were heavy and cumbersome to use, and it took experience to judge just how hot the iron should be for different kinds of fabric. Usually two or more irons were heated on the stove at once and used in rotation.

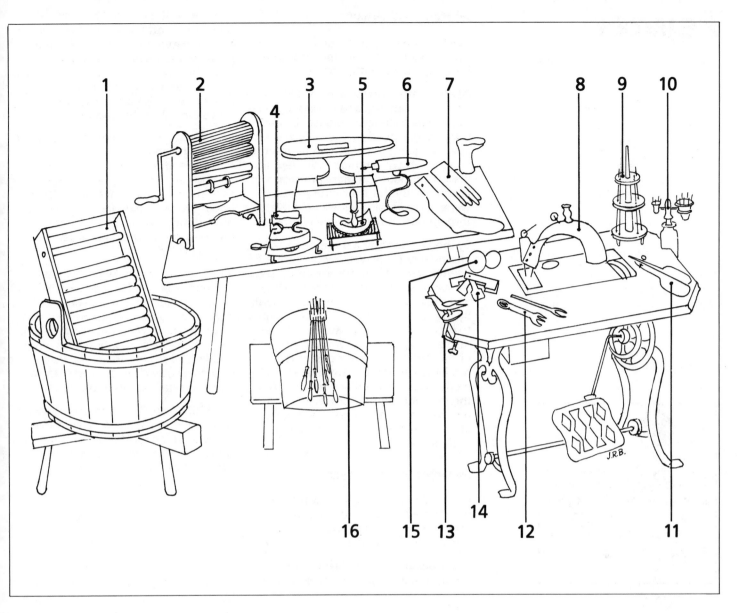

Washing and Ironing Tools

1. Wash Tub and Board: Clothes were washed and rinsed in wooden tubs. They were rubbed up and down on a corrugated board to scrub the dirt out.

2. Clothes Wringer: Inventors did much to ease the hard job of washing, and many types of wringers were invented in the 19th century.

3. Sleeve Board: Small ironing board for ironing shirt sleeves.

4. Box Iron: Box irons differed from the solid-cast "sadirons" in that they had a hollow core in which a hot iron "slug" was placed.

5. Fluting Iron: For ironing ruffles and flounces in fashionable clothes. The starched material to be "fluted" was placed on the corrugated block and a corrugated iron pressed it.

6. Goffering Iron: Also used to make ruffles, this type of iron was heated with a hot iron rod inserted in the "tube."

7. Sock and Glove Stretchers: Laundered socks and gloves were dried and stretched on these.

Needlecraft Tools

8. Sewing Machine: Sewing machines greatly eased home sewing and revolutionized the textile industry. Hundreds of models were patented in the second half of the 19th century. This one was patented in 1858 by Major Samuel Comfort of Bucks County, Pennsylvania.

9. Spool Rack: Racks (or "reels") to hold thread were a necessity. This one is homemade.

10. Knitting Frame: Used to make knitted strips for belts, suspenders, etc.

11. Rug Hook: A semi-automatic hook called a "shuttle hooker" for making hooked rugs.

12. Shuttles: These were used for weaving on small "tape looms" and in netting thread or twine to make shawls, hair nets, bed canopies, and hammocks.

13. Sewing Bird: An ornate clamp that held fabric and rug braids taut while they were being worked on.

14. Button Hole Cutter: Tool with five blades for cutting different sized button holes.

15. Darning Gourds: Gourds made practical "eggs" on which to darn (mend) knitted socks and mittens.

16. Lace Pillow and Bobbin: Used to make "bobbin" or "pillow" lace. Threads were attached by pins to the cushion and each thread was wound on a bobbin. By crossing the bobbins over and under each other in intricate patterns, the threads turned around the pins, forming the various meshes of the lace.

Pewter

History of Pewter

Pewter is an alloy composed of tin and small amounts of other metals such as lead, copper, bismuth, and zinc.

Pewter was known to the ancient Chinese, Egyptians, and Greeks, but was not widely produced because tin was scarce and expensive. The alloy was first made in quantities in Britain during the late Roman era. Abundant tin deposits made its production there practical and profitable. By the 3rd century, pewter wares were in fairly widespread use throughout Roman-occupied Europe.

By the 13th century, a great demand had arisen among the wealthy of Europe for pewter wares. Until the late 1500's, pewter was used primarily by the wealthy and the church (for ceremonial vessels). By the 17th century, the rich had begun to prefer silver and glassware on their tables, and pewter became a commodity of the middle and lower classes. It almost totally replaced the many utensils formerly made of wood and horn. During the mid-18th century, porcelain and pottery began to replace pewter in European households and its production declined.

Pewter in America

From 1725 to 1825, pewter was the most widely used metal in America. A great variety of vessels were made for home, church, and tavern use.

It is probable that the first colonists brought pewter spoons, dishes, and pots along with them to the New World. As pewter is a soft metal, and wares made from it are easily damaged, the need for pewterers to mend these wares existed from the days of the earliest settlements. The first known pewterer to come to America was Richard Graves, who arrived in Salem, Massachusetts in 1635.

Lack of raw tin hampered colonial pewtering. England placed heavy taxes on tin exported to America, forcing the early pewterers to rely on old pewter for their production of new wares: they bought broken and worn-out pieces, melted them down, and re-cast them into new forms. The bulk of new pewter was imported.

Some of the famous American pewterers working from 1750 to 1850 were William Will of Philadelphia, the Bassetts of New York, and the Danforths and Boardmans of Connecticut. Most pewterers sold directly from their workshops and hired peddlers to sell in rural areas. Large shops sold great quantities of pewter to wholesale and retail outlets in other cities.

By 1850, cheap silverplate and boneware had begun to replace pewter in the home, and the third quarter of the 19th century saw the end of pewter as a domestic ware.

Pewter Wares

Pictured are examples of most of the principal stock forms of pewter made and used in America.

Coffeepots

Coffeepots were not made until after 1750. They reached the height of their popularity between 1825 and 1850. Most were made of a metal called Britannia, a fine pewter with no lead.

Teapots

The first type of teapot made in America was the so-called Queen Anne type, with pear-shaped body and wooden handle. They were made from about 1750 to 1800. The other teapots exhibited show later designs.

Tankards and Mugs

Tankards are one-handled, covered drinking vessels. Their lids were either dome-shaped or flat. During the 18th century, tankards were gradually replaced by the open-topped mug.

Lighting Devices

Pewter was used for almost every type of lighting device in the late 18th and early 19th centuries. Exhibited are candlesticks, whale oil lamps, and fluid lamps.

Plates and Dishes

Plates, used to hold individual portions of food, were shallow and seldom exceeded 10" in diameter. Plates over 10" were called dishes and were used to distribute food at the table. Plates and dishes, along with basins, made up the bulk of the pewterer's trade.

Basins

Basins are bowl-shaped containers that were used to hold puddings, stews, and other semi-liquid foods. Five standard sizes were made.

Porringers

Small bowls used to hold food, porringers were popular throughout the 19th century. Only rarely has a two-handled porringer been found; most surviving specimens have one. Handles were of two types: the solid handle, inherited from Continental Europe; and the English type, which was pierced, or "flowered."

Pit Sawing

Pit Saws are long two-man saws which were used to saw planks from logs.

They were called Pit Saws because the timber being sawn was usually placed over a pit or convenient hollow in the ground, or it was extended out from the side of a hill. One sawyer (called the "pitman") stood below, pulling the saw, which cut only on the downstroke, towards him. The other worker (known as the "tiller" or top sawyer) stood above, right on the log. He pulled the long blade up after a cut had been made. A wedge placed in the split prevented the blade from getting stuck midway through a stroke.

Pit sawing is an ancient method of sawing wood. It was used in the Orient and in Europe for many centuries prior to the full development of water power and sawmill technology. Because pit sawing was such slow and laborious work (two men could cut only about 200 feet of lumber in a day), it was not ever as widely practiced in America as sawing with the "Up-and-Down" Sawmill. Pit sawing was generally used in this country only in new settlements or where it was not practical or feasible to build a sawmill. The sawmill was essentially a pit saw heavily framed in wood and run by water instead of man power.

Printing

Colonial printers turned out their news sheets, pamphlets, "almanacks," and an occasional book on hand presses which differed little from the press on which Johannes Gutenberg printed his first book around 1450. The working parts of colonial presses were of iron, but the heavy framework was made of wood. Later presses, like the museum's flatbed press made c. 1830 by the R. Hoe Company of New York, were made entirely of iron.

There were usually two kinds of workmen in a printing office: compositors and pressmen. Compositors arranged the lead letters on "composing sticks," then placed the finished text on a flat metal "galley" so a "proof" could be made. After corrections in the galley had been made, the type was securely wedged in an iron frame called a "chase." The chase fit into the bed of the press which slid beneath the heavy iron "platen" by means of a hand crank and rollers. The pressmen operated the press. One inked the type with a roller, and another placed the clean sheet of paper in the press, cranked the bed under the platen, and brought the platen down by means of a lever to make an impression.

Presses like this one were in general use until superceded by the cylinder press in the 1860's. They were, however, used to print broadsides as late as 1910.

Pottery Making

The tools and techniques of low fire or "redware" pottery production changed very little during the two thousand years preceding the 20th century. Redware was commonly used in America for everyday crockery. Bowls, jugs, dishes, jars, milk pans, colanders, pitchers, and so on were made of redware until the mid-19th century when tinware and more durable kinds of pottery became readily available.

Clay Preparation

Clay occurs naturally wherever wind or water has deposited quantities of fine silt. Most clays have iron in them which gives the characteristic red color. The potter dug clay from a deposit, dried it, separated stones from it, and put it in a barrel-shaped **pug mill.** The shaft of the mill was turned by an animal. Short blades extended from the shaft so that as water was slowly added to the dry clay, a smooth, elastic clay was formed.

Glazes

Glazes were made from a combination of water, quartz or flint, a white clay (al-though red would work), and a metallic mineral which imparted color. Red lead was most commonly used for a clear glaze, manganese gave black, and copper gave green. The dry materials were ground together in a **glaze mill** until they were fine. Water was added so they could be applied to dried pots. The glaze mill looked and operated like a quern for grinding cereal grains.

The Kiln

The finished pots were stacked in a **kiln,** a large dome-shaped structure built of brick and stone. A kiln might hold a thousand pots or more, so it was only fired once or twice a year. Pots were stacked inside (often on special supports or "kiln furniture" to separate them), the doorway was sealed, and fires were started in fireboxes built into the base of the kiln. The fires were tended continuously for about 18 to 24 hours—until the pottery reached the proper temperature (about 1800°F.). After a day or two of cooling, the finished pots were removed from the kiln.

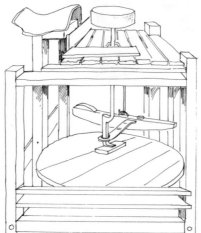

The Potter's Wheel

Hollow ware—jugs, bowls, cups, pitchers, and pots—were made on a potter's wheel. The potter sat at or stood by the wheel, and with his foot he moved a lever that drove a flywheel attached to a wheel on top of a flat work space. A piece of clay was placed on this wheel, and as it turned, the potter shaped it with his hand into the desired form.

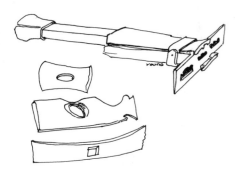

Ribs and Extruders

While the potter could simply smooth and shape his wheel-thrown pots with his hands or a wet cloth, a smoother and more precise surface could be achieved by using a wooden rib. Ribs were made in a variety of shapes. Some simply served to smooth pots, but some were shaped so as to form lips, rims, or even to act as templates for the insides or outsides of pots.

Handles could be stretched from a roll of clay, or they could be made with an extruder. Soft clay was placed inside the hollow tube of the extruder after a wooden pattern of the proper size and shape had been put on the end. A piston-like handle forced the clay out through the pattern, making a long strip that could be cut into desired lengths for handles.

Drape Mold Pottery

Plates, saucers, and platters were made on molds rather than on the wheel. Prepared clay was draped over wooden or ceramic forms which would shape it. These molded pieces were often decorated with either a "slip decoration," a scratched or "sgraffito" decoration, or a combination of both. Slip was a creamy mixture of colored clay and water. Most slip is made from white clay, though the lead glazes make it seem yellow. Beautiful effects could be achieved by covering the entire surface of a piece with slip and then scraping it away in some places to reveal the red clay. Often colored glazes were dabbed or painted on these fancier pieces.

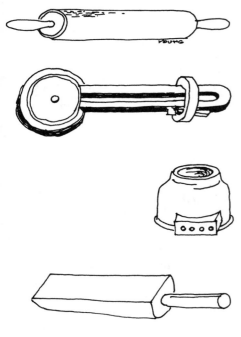

Clay to be drape molded was first rolled out with a **roller** to a uniform thickness. Road dust might be collected and used, as bakers do flour, to keep the moist clay from sticking to the roller.

The rolled clay was cut into a circle of the desired size with a **potter's compass**. The flat surface of the compass rested on the clay, and a small blade sliced through the clay. Wooden templates might be used for plates and platters of unusual shape.

Slip—clay mixed with water until it was as runny as cream—was applied to the plate with a **slip trailer**. Goose quills served as spouts in these little pitcher-like tools. Many had several spouts, and some were divided so that two colors might be applied at once.

When the slip dried a little, but before the clay disk or "bat" had gotten hard, the design was beaten into the surface with a **tamper**. Besides smoothing the design, this helped assure a good bond between the two kinds of clay.

After tamping, the edge was "coggled" with a **coggle wheel**. Redware is quite fragile, so besides providing a decorative edge, coggling helped prevent noticeable chipping around the rim.

While the decorated bat was still moist, it was draped over a **mold** of the desired shape and size. Smoothing the clay over the mold was enough to make it hold the proper shape. The finished piece was then set on a board to dry before it was glazed and fired.

Press Molds and Slip Molds

Clay was pressed by hand onto a plaster press mold so that an impression was made. With the clay still on the mold, the pot was shaped. For circular pots, the mold was put right on the wheel so that the unmolded part of the pot could be smoothed. After shaping, the pot was removed from the mold.

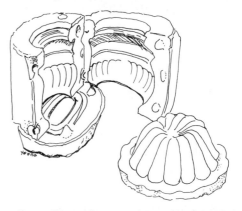

Slip molds are frequently made of several pieces. The parts of the mold were tied together, and the mold was filled up with a thick slip made of clay and water. The plaster of the mold drew enough moisture from the slip so that when it was poured out of the mold, a layer of clay would be left, evenly coating the mold. After the clay had dried a bit, the mold could be removed.

Recreation: Toys, Sports & Amusements

Scientific and Educational Toys

Tremendous advances were being made in all branches of science in the 19th century, particularly in the knowledge and application of optics and in the new science of photography. As a result, "Optical Toys," the precursors of television and motion pictures, were manufactured and sold in great quantities for family entertainment.

Magic Lanterns: These were the first slide projectors. They were made in England, France, Germany, and America throughout the 19th century. A magic lantern consists of the metal lantern body, an internal light source, and a system of lenses and mirrors for projecting transparent images painted on glass "slides" onto a screen or wall. Magic lanterns were a source of delight and education for the entire family during the Victorian era.

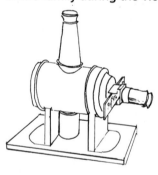

Stereoscopes: The stereoscope is a device that gives a striking three-dimensional effect to pictures viewed through it. The earliest "stereo views" were painted pictures; almost all of the ones produced in the second half of the 19th century were photographs printed on cardboard. Stereo views depicted almost every imaginable subject and were produced in vast quantities.

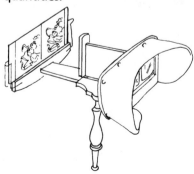

Peep Shows: Peep Shows contained a three-dimensional scene or group of objects which was viewed through a small opening or lens. Highly artistic and intricate peep shows were popular attractions at fairs and festivals during the 18th century. Later, smaller, less elaborate ones were produced for home use.

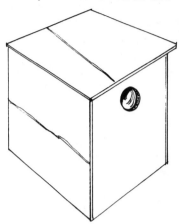

Electricity Generators: Static electricity generators were first used by scientists in the 18th century to produce electricity for study purposes. By the 19th century they were found in American homes, where they were used to demonstrate the laws of the "new" phenomena of electricity and to perform curious and entertaining electrical experiments.

Toys and Play in 18th Century America

Play in colonial America, particularly in Puritan New England, was frowned upon, but children still had fun. They played some of the same games that children today play—like ball, tag, hopscotch, hide-and-seek, and jump rope. They also had crudely carved wooden dolls and toys. By 1700 a few English toys were being imported and craftsmen and farmers had begun to make toys in their spare time. It was not long before the making of wooden toys had become a sideline for carpenters and wood carvers. By 1800 toys of tin, glass, pottery, and

even pewter were being produced by craftsmen in addition to their regular line of work.

19th Century Toys

Wooden Toys: Until about 1840 wood was the most widely used material for toys. In Pennsylvania German areas, where traditional toymaking skills had been brought from Germany, the toy center of Europe, more wooden toys were produced than anywhere else in the country. The variety of wooden toys included dolls and doll houses, sets of miniature furniture, boats, wagons, figures of people and animals, tops, hoops, inter-

locking puzzles, building blocks, Noah's Arks (a great favorite), rocking horses, checkers, and dominoes.

Tin Toys: In the second half of the 19th century tin toys were produced in prolific numbers. Because it was light, easily shaped, and inexpensive, tin was an ideal material for toys. There were toy pails and buckets, teapots and utensils, pencil boxes and doll house furniture. Tin pull-toys and wind-up (spring-operated) toys became very popular. One manufacturer is known to have produced 40 million tin toys annually in the 1870's.

Cast Iron Toys: Toys made of cast iron appeared in the mid-19th century. Great numbers of iron pull-toys—colorfully painted animals and figures on wheels—were manufactured. Little cast iron stoves complete with pots, pans, and skillets were popular with girls; the perennial favorite of boys was the iron transportation model—farm and circus wagons, sailing vessels and steamships, fire engines, trolley cars, and trains.

Dolls and Doll Houses: 19th century children continued to enjoy homemade dolls of rag, cornhusk, and wood, but as the century progressed dolls became more elaborate. Papier maché doll heads were imported early in the century. Painted heads from Austria and Germany came next, followed by wax doll heads from England. The heads were attached to linen, canvas, or leather doll bodies dressed in the latest fashions.

Doll houses filled with tiny furnishings had been popular in Europe since the 16th century. They reached the height of their popularity in America during the Victorian era. Doll houses of all kinds and sizes, both home- and factory-made, were available to rich and poor children alike. The making of doll house furnishings was a lucrative sideline for many craftsmen.

Games and Sports in 19th Century America

A whole new world of recreational pastimes opened up in the years following the Civil War for the average American man, woman, and child. Despite a 12-14 hour workday and the continuing influence of the Puritan ethic that frowned upon "frivolous amusements," Americans became very serious about learning how to play. "Physical Culture" was the name given to this new obsession with adult games and sports.

Grown women began escaping the kitchen and parlor for such "lady-like" pursuits as croquet, archery, lawn tennis, bowling, and ice skating. "Manly" sports included polo, cricket, football, riflery, fox hunting,

horseshoe pitching, trotting races, boxing, fencing, and baseball. By the 1880's baseball had become the most popular sport in the country and America was on its way to becoming the greatest sporting nation in the world.

By 1870 energetic outdoor activities were being recommended for children, especially for the children of the ever-increasing number of city dwellers. Popular outdoor games and sports of children included cup-and-ball, battledore and shuttlecock (a game similar to badminton), stilt-walking, rope-jumping, kite-flying, baseball, croquet, ice skating and sledding, marbles, and top-spinning.

The Bicycle

The American craze for bicycling began in the 1880's with the invention of the "safety bicycle." Here was rapid, cheap, and fun transportation for all. The "drop-frame" bicycle for ladies played a major role in releasing American women from the rigid codes of "proper" behavior they were accustomed to, by getting them outdoors and into active sports with no loss of dignity or modesty. The bicycle prepared the way for the automobile industry by making Americans want to travel and it was a prime factor in the building of hard-topped roads. The U.S. Census Bureau, at the turn of the 20th century, stated that few articles ever created had caused such a change in the lives of ordinary people as had the bicycle.

Puppets and Marionettes

The art of puppetry has been traced back to nearly all the great nations of antiquity and is possibly man's oldest form of dramatic representation. The puppet show reached Europe in the early years of the Christian era and by the 18th century it held a position not far below that of the theatre itself in public popularity and esteem.

Puppetry was a favorite entertainment in colonial America. Roving puppeteers put on shows in taverns, at fairs, and on village greens. In the 19th century puppet shows were featured in city theatres and were welcomed in remote areas as great events. Puppet showmen roamed the frontier, putting on shows wherever an audience could be found. Punch and

his battered wife Judy were the reigning stars of the puppet stage.

Marionettes are puppets moved by strings or wires. The marionette theatre reached its greatest perfection in Italy, and many of the great puppet showmen of Europe and America were Italian.

Shingle Making

An Important Rural Industry

The production of shingles was an important aspect of rural technology in America until well into the 19th century. Shingles were used to roof the numerous buildings that were part of a functioning farm and were widely used on homes and businesses in urban centers.

Shingle making was a major home industry which was pursued by men and boys everywhere. It was one of many winter tasks which were necessary for farm building and maintenance. Roofing with shingles—from selecting the proper wood in the forest to nailing or pegging the finished product in place— required special skills that were usually taught to male farm children by their fathers or grandfathers.

Shingles were not only used domestically; they were one of America's first exported products. From the early 17th century on shingles (along with boards and barrel staves) were collected in port towns and shipped to markets in Europe and the West Indies. In the three-year period from 1771-1773, for example, almost 60 million shingles were sent from the colonies to the West Indies. Philadelphia served as one of the major ports from which shingles and other forest products were shipped.

Shingles were made from a variety of woods. In Pennsylvania the preferred wood was white oak, which grew in abundance. Elsewhere, favored woods were chestnut, cedar, cypress, pine, and ash. Most shingled roofs needed replacing after about 30 years, but a well-shingled and maintained roof could last up to 60 years.

By 1850, the hand-splitting and shaving of shingles was a fast declining tradition. By 1900, milled (sawn) shingles and other roofing materials such as slate and tin had all but replaced handmade shingles.

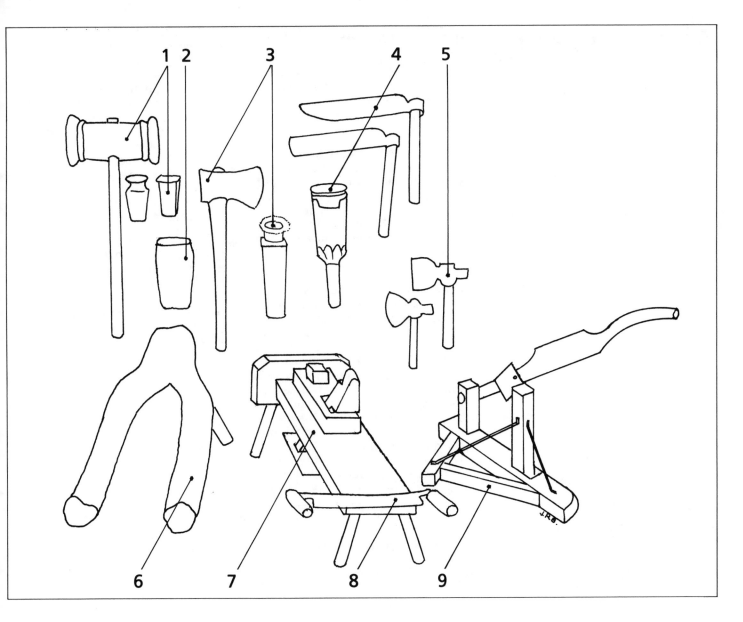

Shingle Making Tools

1. Beetle and Iron Wedge: Used to split lengths of logs into bolts (halves and then quarters) prior to their being rived (split) into shingles.

2. Wooden Wedge: Also known as a "glut," this hardwood wedge was used to release an iron wedge from a log by widening the split.

3. Split Axe and Wooden Headed Wedges: The wedge-shaped, dull-bladed split axe (or holzaxt) was used to split small logs. It was also used, in conjunction with a wooden-headed wedge, as an alternative to the beetle and iron wedge. These wedges have wooden heads because the iron split axe would have ruined an iron wedge by causing its top to spread.

4. Froe and Froe Maul: Used to split shingles from a bolt of wood. The froe was placed on top of the bolt and repeatedly struck with the wooden maul (club) along its blade until the shingle split away from the block of wood.

5. Shingling Hatchets: Specialized factory-produced hatchets produced after 1840. Used to split, trim, nail on, and remove shingles.

6. Froe Horse: Also known as a "brake" or "buck", this homemade apparatus held a bolt of wood while it was being split. Placed vertically in the crotch, the bolt was prevented from slipping or falling over.

7. Shaving Horse: Bench on which the shingle maker sat while shaving shingles with his drawknife. A foot-operated clamp held the shingle firmly so the worker had both hands free.

8. Drawknife: Two-handled knife used to shave and trim shingles.

9. Shingle Butter: Used to trim the rough, uneven butt (lower) ends of shaved shingles.

Shoemaking

Shoes Throughout History

The moccasin is probably the oldest type of shoe. Sandals, made of materials such as leather, straw, rushes, and wood, were the common shoe worn by peoples of ancient Egypt, China, India, Greece, and Rome.

During the Middle Ages, the open-toed sandal was replaced in Europe by clumsy shoes made of leather or wood which were designed to hide the foot, and which had no distinction between right and left. In 1670 the shoe buckle appeared, and throughout the 18th century buckles were a conspicuous and ever-present ornament on shoes.

Heavy, boxy-looking shoes called "batts" were worn in America until the end of the 18th century by men, women, and children alike. They had stubby heels and thick soles which were often studded with hobnails to make them last longer. These shoes were held on by two straps called latchets which crossed over the tongue and were held together with a buckle or leather string. The first shoes to open in front and lace with a shoestring were made in New England about 1790. During the 19th century, boots were the most popular footwear for men and boys. Women and girls wore "gaiters," ankle-high shoes fastened with lacings or buttons up the side.

Shoemaking in America

The first shoemaker in America, an Englishman named Thomas Beard, arrived in Salem, Massachusetts in 1629. Others soon followed. These early shoemakers travelled from village to village, staying at each house as long as it took to make shoes for the entire family. The demand for their services became so great that soon they began to set up shop in their homes. Around 1700 the first shoe stores appeared, followed by shoe factories where large numbers of apprentices and journeymen were employed. Shoes were ordered and custom-made to fit one customer. By 1750 shoemakers had begun to make ready-made, or "sale shoes," for display in their shops and for export.

By 1776 shoemaking was well-established on a commercial basis, and by 1791 an estimated 8 million pairs of shoes were being made annually. By the mid-19th century the shoe and boot industry employed more workers than any other branch of American industry.

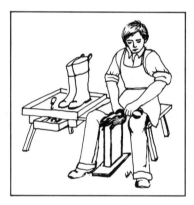

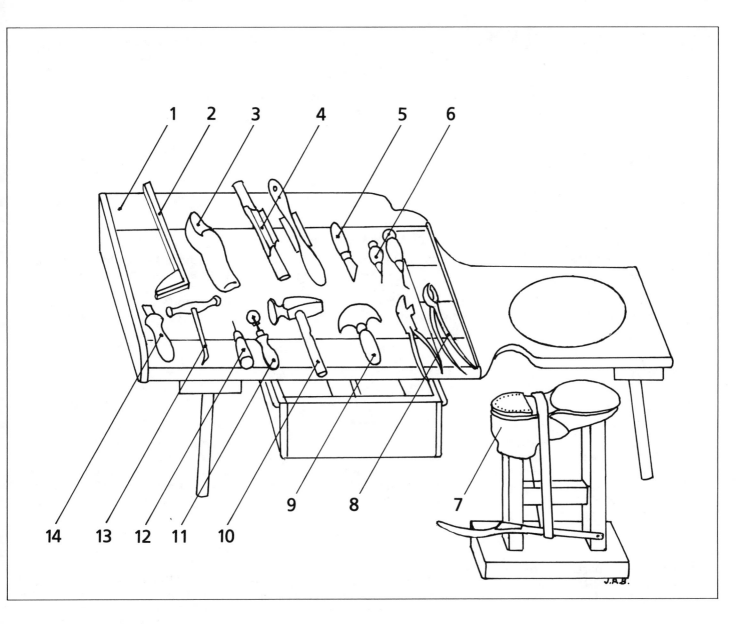

Shoemaking Tools

1. Bench: Seat on which the shoemaker sat while assembling a shoe. Drawers, compartments, and leather straps provided convenient storage for his tools.

2. Size Stick: Marked rule for measuring the size and contours of a customer's foot.

3. Shoe Last: Hand-carved model of a customer's foot. The shoe was shaped and assembled on the last.

4. Drawknives: Sharp-bladed tools used to carve the last from a block of wood.

5. Clicking Knife: Used to cut the "uppers" of the shoe (the uppers consisted of two pieces of leather known as the counter and the vamp).

6. Clicker's Awls: Used to punch holes in the uppers, which were then sewn together with waxed thread.

7. Lasting Jack: Standing vise which held the shoe while it was being assembled on the last.

8. Lasting Pincers: Curved pliers used to pull the uppers tightly around the last before they were tacked down securely.

9. Sole Knife: Sharp knife shaped like a half-moon, used to cut a rough sole from thick cowhide.

10. Hammer: Used to pound the thick sole leather (which had been soaked for several hours in water) to make it softer and more pliable.

11. Marking Wheel: After a narrow groove had been cut around the sole, close to the edge, this tool was used to mark each point through which the thread connecting sole to upper would pass.

12. Sole Awl: Used to punch holes in the sole at each point marked by the wheel.

13. Last Hook: After the shoe had been assembled and trimmed, the last was removed from the jack, and the shoe was removed from the last using this hook.

14. Burnisher: Heated and used to rub the edges of sole and heel to a hard and glossy finish.

Textile Fibers

Flax

Egyptian tomb paintings indicate that the complicated process of making the flax plant into linen thread has changed little during the last 5000 years. In early America, most families had a small plot of flax. In April, flaxseed was sown thickly to insure tall, straight plants. In July, the plants were pulled up by their roots, the seeds were removed, and the flax was prepared for "retting," a process of vegetable decay. Bundles of flax were soaked in a pond or slow-moving stream for about six weeks to rot the waste vegetable material from the fiber.

The **rippler** was usually made of a single row of strong spikes or comb-like teeth. It was attached to a bench, and the freshly harvested flax was drawn through the rippler to remove the seeds.

A special **flail** was used by the Germans of Pennsylvania instead of a rippler. Seed was ground at oil mills into feed and linseed oil, one of America's earliest commercial products.

After the retted flax had dried, the stem was cracked with the **brake.** A small bundle of flax was placed across the lower blades and the upper ones broke the straw-like chaff from the fibers.

The loose pieces of stem were removed from the fiber with the **scutching knife.** The flax was laid on a vertical board and was struck with the sword-like knife until it was clean and smooth.

The **hatchel** separated the long fibers and removed the short ones which were called "tow." The tow from the coarse hatchel was used for bags and ropes; from the finer hatchel, for work clothes.

The hatchelled flax was wound onto the **distaff** so that a few strands at a time could be spun together into fine linen thread. Decorated distaffs and hatchels were often given as engagement gifts.

Wool

Sheep's wool is probably man's most ancient textile fiber. It is durable, warm, fireproof, and easy to dye. It provided Spain and later England with the wealth to build empires. In America, it was commonly spun at home as late as the Civil War.

While sheep may not like getting sheared, it does not hurt them. All breeds of sheep have different types of wool. Some wool is short and springy and is suitable for being carded and spun into airy woolen yarns. Some is long and straight and is best for combing and spinning into strong worsted thread. Wool might be "spun in the grease," but usually the dirt and oil (lanolin) were washed from the fleece with strong lye.

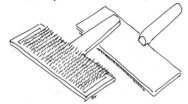

Children often prepared wool for spinning with **cards.** A bit of wool placed between two cards could be untangled, fluffed, and finally rolled into a loose coil called a "rolag."

Wool combs were difficult to use. A comb with wool on it was attached to a post. Carefully swinging another comb through the wool produced a rope of wool called a "sliver" which was used for worsted thread.

Cotton, Hemp, and Silk

Almost no cotton was grown in America before 1800. Before that time, it was commonly imported from the West Indies for home spinning. The smooth seeds of West Indian cotton were easy to remove, and the cotton could be carded like wool, though cotton cards are usually larger and finer than wool cards. Cotton was popular because it was soft, comfortable, and it could be easily colored. Hemp was a very common early American crop. It was processed like flax, and it was used for making rope and sacks. Silk was produced in America, but the amount of time needed to "reel" it and imperfect knowledge of silk-reeling kept it from being common.

Spinning

Drop Spindles

One of man's earliest discoveries was that twisting fibers while gently drawing them away from each other produced yarn. The drop spindle, the most ancient example of the flywheel, solved the problems of how to provide constant twist, how to provide even draw, and where to store the yarn that had been spun. It was

made of some kind of weight or "whorl" and a shaft that had a hook or groove for the fibers to catch on. Each culture had its own types of drop spindles.

When the spindle was spun and dropped, fibers held between the fingers and caught on the hook could be easily drawn out into yarn so long as the spindle kept spinning and did not reach the ground. When the spindle stopped, the yarn could be wound around it and the process could be continued.

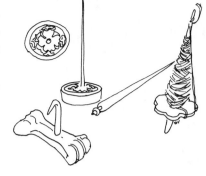

The Spindle

The drop spindle was common everywhere in the world until at least the 18th century, but in Europe spindle-type wheels were introduced from the Orient during the Middle Ages.

The spindle-type wheel had a simple drop

spindle laid on its side and held between two uprights by pieces of leather or straw. A drive cord passed around the whorl. This arrangement allowed for smoother turning of the whorl, more even draw, and greater speed. The spindle-type wheel provided a better yarn more quickly than the drop spindle.

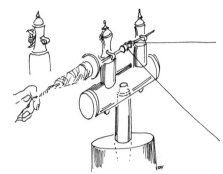

Spindle-Type Wheel

The spindle-type wheel was commonly used in Europe and America for spinning wool. The spinster held the wool rolag or sliver in the left hand and turned the drive wheel with the right hand or with a short piece of wood called a "wool finger." The fiber passed through a groove on the tip of the spindle which held it while the spinster drew out the yarn with

a backwards step or two. When the draw was complete, the spinster freed the yarn from the tip of the spindle and turned the drivewheel to wind the newly-spun yarn onto the shaft of the spindle.
A piece of cornhusk placed on the shank of the spindle made it easy to slip off the cone-shaped "cop" of yarn that accumulated on the spindle. A spinster might expect to spin a pound of wool into a piece of yarn several miles long.

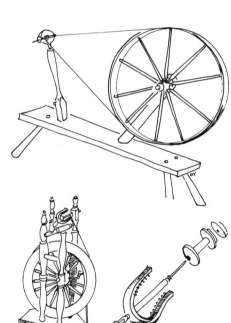

The Flyer

During the Renaissance in Europe the flyer was developed as an improvement over the spindle. The flyer assembly consisted of a bobbin for storing spun yarn which was driven by one pulley and a U-shaped flyer that was driven at a sightly slower speed by another pulley. Fibers were twisted at the mouth of the orifice drilled in the end of the flyer, and the

spun yarn was wound onto the bobbin by the flyer. The hooks on the flyer arm helped to distribute the yarn evenly.

The flyer allowed yarn to be continuously spun and wound onto the bobbin. The spinster had only to stop to move the yarn to another hook now and then. When the bobbin was full, it could be easily removed and stored until the yarn was wound into skeins.

Flyer-Type Wheel

The addition of the treadle allowed the spinster to pedal the flywheel with her foot so that both hands could be used to draw out the yarn in front of the orifice.

Flax was commonly spun on flyer-type wheels, although they work well for any other type of fiber. There is often a place

on the saddle of the wheel for a distaff to hold the flax, and frequently a small container for water can be found with the wheel. Spinsters wet their fingers while spinning flax to dissolve its natural gums a bit. If a spinster was very skilled, she might spin with two hands at once on a wheel with two flyers and so produce twice as much!

Winding and Weaving

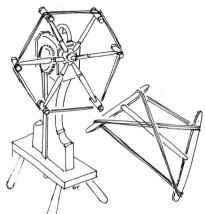

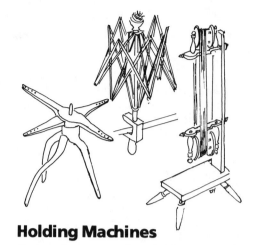

Measuring Tools

When a spinster had finished a cop or a bobbin, the yarn was wound into loose skeins of prescribed lengths. In America wool was usually wound in 840 yard "hanks" and linen in 300 yard "cuts."

The **clock or click reel** had a set of gears that recorded each revolution of the arms. After a certain number of turns—usually 40—the gears activated a springy piece of wood that made a loud "click."

The **niddy noddy** was another convenient measuring tool. It was held in the middle, and a set length of yarn—usually 2 yards—was measured in each revolution.

Holding Machines

Skeins of yarn were frequently washed or dyed after spinning, and that caused some shrinkage. Holding machines had to be adjustable so as to hold various sized skeins while they were unwound for other purposes.

These machines were usually called **swifts.** Some were quite simple, having only a few adjustable sticks on an axle. Others, like the **squirrel cage swift** (or rice) were quite elaborate. The **umbrella swift** folded up for convenient storage.

Winding Machines

A weaver had to wind skeined yarn onto some kind of core before it could be used. Yarn that was going to be put in a shuttle and used as weft was wound onto small bobbins, cornhusks, or goose quills. Yarn for warp was often wound onto spools.

The **quilling machine** or spool winder had a spindle that held either a quill or a spool. A crank on the flywheel powered the spindle, and yarn could be quickly wound off of skeins.

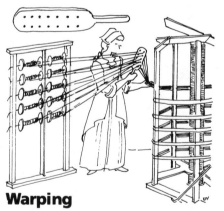

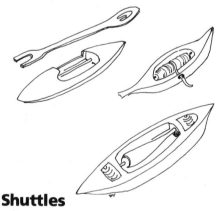

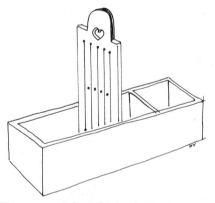

Warping

Spools of warp yarn set in a frame-like **creel** could be prepared for weaving with a **warping mill,** a large rigid frame with four or more sides that turned on a central axis. Having determined the number of revolutions for winding the length of one warp thread, the weaver could wind many threads at once onto the mill by threading the yarn through a **warping paddle.** Usually the entire warp was wound on the mill before it was put on the loom. Pegs set in a wall could serve the same function as a mill, but not as effectively.

Shuttles

Shuttles hold the weft thread that is passed from one side of the separated warp threads (the "shed") to the other. The **boat shuttle** is most common, as its shape allowed it to pass freely through the shed and permitted the weft yarn wound on quills or small bobbins to unwind freely. **Fly shuttles** were cast through the shed by a mechanism, and they have protective metal tips. **Net needles** were used with tape looms where the weaver could simply pass the shuttle from hand to hand rather than throwing it and catching it through a wide shed.

Tape or Rigid Heddle Looms

Narrow bands, belts, fringe, and ribbons were made on **tape looms.** Some tape looms have reels to hold warp threads and finished tape, some just have a single warp reel, and some required the weaver to tie one end of the warp to a chair and the other around his or her waist. Even so, they all work in more or less the same way. Alternate warp threads passed through slits and holes in a "heddle board." One shed was formed when the threads in slits were lifted above the ones in holes; the other when they were lowered. In spite of its simplicity, beautiful tapes were made on these looms.

Loom

A loom is a frame for making cloth. It holds the warp threads that will run the length of the cloth straight and even, and it has a mechanism to help form a space or "shed" for the shuttle to pass through with the weft thread. On most 18th and 19th century looms, the warp threads were stored on a roller at the back of the loom. They passed forward through string loops or "heddles" attached to frames or "harnesses" that were moved with pedals. From the heddles, each warp thread passed through a comb-like "reed" or beater before it was tied to a roller that held woven cloth.

For plain weave, two harnesses were needed. The first thread was put through a heddle in one harness; the second, through a heddle in the other. All odd threads went into the first harness; all even ones, in the second. When the first harness was lifted, all of the odd threads lifted, forming a shed for the weft thread to pass through. The reed beat the thread into place, and the other harness could be lifted for the next weft thread. A weaver might weave three yards of cloth in a long day's work.

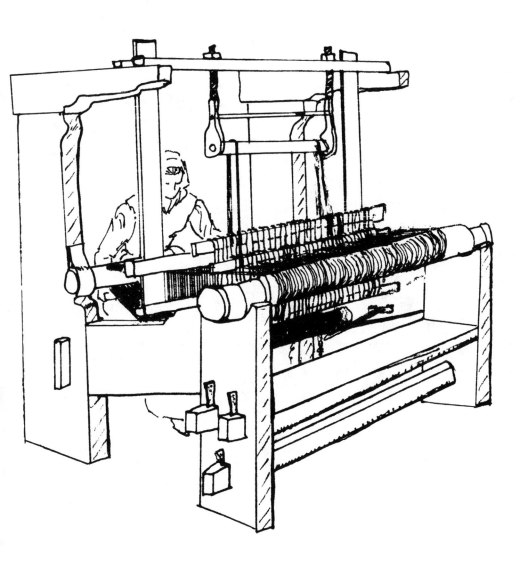

Stoves and Firebacks

Five-Plate Stoves and Firebacks

Five-Plate or Jamb Stoves were the first heating stoves used in America.

The stoves were made of five heavy cast iron stoveplates which were often decorated in relief with biblical pictures and texts. These stoves were brought by German settlers to Pennsylvania in the early 18th century.

Jamb stoves did not have doors or vents in the plates. Instead, a stoke hole and a flue were cut through the back of the kitchen fireplace and the stove was attached to the wall in the adjoining room. Hot coals were shovelled into the stove from the kitchen fireplace, and smoke went out the flue and up the kitchen fireplace chimney.

American production of Five-Plate Stoves covered a span of only about fifty years. By 1770 the more efficient, free-standing Six- and Ten-Plate Stoves were being produced by iron foundries.

Firebacks are iron plates that were leaned or fastened against the back wall of a fireplace to reflect heat out into the room and to protect the masonry at the back of the fireplace. They were often arch-topped, and they were decorated with heraldic or symbolic motifs.

First used in Europe in the 15th century, Firebacks were brought to this country by the English. They were imported from England until American ironworks began making them in the early 18th century.

The enclosed stoves of the Germans and the open fireplaces (often with firebacks) of the English were the two principal heating traditions of early America.

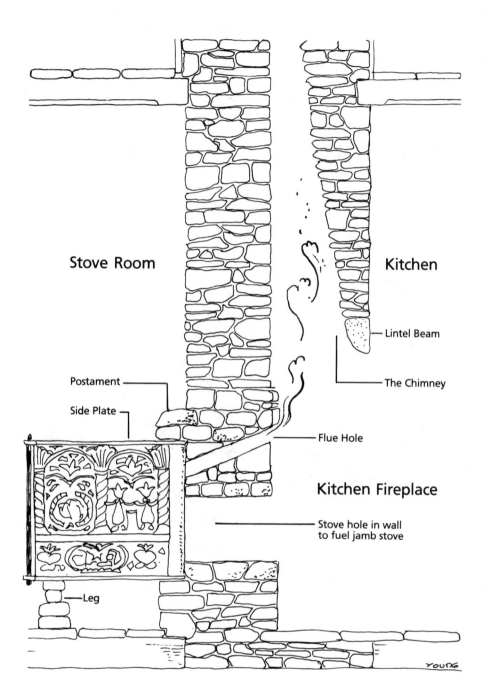

Stove Room

Kitchen

Lintel Beam

The Chimney

Postament

Side Plate

Flue Hole

Kitchen Fireplace

Stove hole in wall to fuel jamb stove

Leg

Six-Plate Stove

The six-plate stove was the first free-standing iron stove.

Also known as "wind," "draft," or Holland stoves, they were constructed of six heavy iron plates cast in open sand. The earliest ones were similar in appearance to the highly-decorated five-plate "jamb" stoves except that a sixth plate covered the back so that the stove could stand free of the wall. The six-plate stove burned wood more efficiently and warmed a room more quickly than the earlier five-plate stove.

Six-plate stoves were in use in northern Europe from at least the mid-1600's, and it is probable that a few were imported to America in the early 1700's. Iron foundries in New York and Pennsylvania were manufacturing these heavy, decorated draft stoves during the mid-1700's. By the late 1700's, these stoves had largely been replaced by smaller, lighter box stoves and ten-plate stoves.

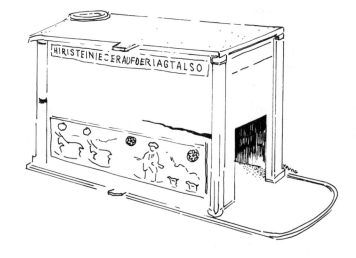

Shaker Stoves

Similar in shape to the six-plate stove, Shaker stoves differed entirely in construction.

Instead of being made of separately-cast plates, Shaker stoves consisted of a firebox cast as a single unit and fitted into a pre-cast bottom plate. The bottom plate extended to form an oval hearth, and the wrought-iron legs were riveted to it. The advantage of the one-piece firebox was that its seamless edge construction prevented escaping sparks, afforded better draft control, and allowed for more efficient wood-burning. Stoves with cast fireboxes were made as early as 1750, but because the Shakers (a religious group that came from England to the northern colonies in 1774) perfected them, stoves of this type are known as Shaker stoves. Like their tools and furniture, the Shakers' stoves were plain and simple and highly functional.

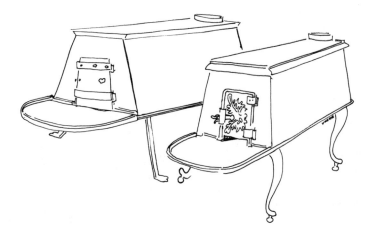

Stoves

Ten-Plate Stoves

Ten-plate stoves were the first effective cooking stoves.

Outwardly, they resemble the earlier six-plate stove, but inside, four cast-iron plates were added to form a rectangular oven above the firebox. The heat and smoke of the fire in the lower chamber passed around the oven from back to front and the smoke left the stove through the hole at the front of the top plate. The fuel door is at the bottom of the front plate, there is a small door at the top for cleaning out soot above the oven, and there are two oven doors, one in each side.

Ten-plate stoves appeared about 1765 in Pennsylvania. They replaced six-plate stoves in popularity, because they both warmed and cooked. The ten-plate stove was used to bake meat, cakes, pies, and bread. It was not equipped to boil, fry, or broil foods. These functions continued to take place in the open-hearth kitchen fireplace until the appearance of cookstoves in the mid-19th century.

Nine-Plate Stoves

So called because they were constructed of nine plates instead of ten, these stoves were popular in the first half of the 19th century.

The front oven plate (of the older ten-plate stove) was eliminated, and the oven was extended forward to the front stove plate. The draft followed the same course as in the ten-plate stove. Called "circular" stoves in furnace records, these stoves were considerably lighter and smaller than ten-plate stoves, and the plates were convex instead of flat. Circular stoves were manufactured and sold in great numbers from New England to the Chesapeake Bay area until about the 3rd quarter of the 19th century.

Column Stove

In the 1840's a new style of stove appeared: the column stove.

This type of stove opened up an entirely new field of design for stove-makers, and between 1843 and 1853, hundreds of patents were issued for imaginative column stoves. Considered the aristocrat of the stove world, they were particularly popular in New York and Pennsylvania. Column stoves gave off an extraordinary amount of heat for the relatively small size of the firebox because the two vertical "towers" radiated twice as much heat as a single flue. The column stove had two front doors which could be opened to give the effect of a fireplace. Between the two columns was a boiling hole, with an ornate cover, over which water could be heated for tea, washing, or shaving.

This stove is a classic example of a column stove. Compact, graceful, and efficient, it was used as a bedroom stove. Its cathedral-like towers and the cross-member connecting them give the stove a Gothic appearance.

Parlor Cookstove

The desire to combine two functions— heating and stovetop cooking—led to the development of the parlor cookstove in the mid-1840's.

The box stove was made wider, and two boiling holes, covered by iron lids, were made in the top plate. In the last half of the 19th century, hundreds of styles of parlor stoves were manufactured and marketed. They were often very ornate and the cooking holes were almost always hidden, when not in use, by a removable cover topped with an ornamental urn. This parlor cookstove has a cooking surface of two lids, under which is a large oven. It burned either wood or coal. On the extended hearth is the ashpit door with a sliding draft control. The stoking door is on the side.

The parlor cookstove gradually evolved into the cooking range with four or more cooking holes and was moved from the parlor into the kitchen. Placed in the kitchen fireplace, the cooking range put an end to open-hearth cooking in America.

Surveying and Navigation

Science in Early America

The ability to measure land—surveying—and to accurately direct a ship's course—navigation—was an important aspect of territorial and economic expansion in colonial America. Surveyors defined the bounds of private property and the boundaries of colonies and future states. Navigators established trade routes along the coastal and inland waterways as well as with the rest of the world. These men, along with the cartographers who explored and mapped the wilderness, the craftsmen who made their tools, and the teachers who trained men to undertake these tasks, were America's first practical scientists.

Land expansion and trade increased rapidly during the 17th century, and there was an increasing need for men with knowledge of surveying and navigation. Colonial schools emphasized practical mathematics, and subjects such as surveying, navigation, geography, and astronomy were regular features of the school curriculum until well into the 19th century.

The Instrument Makers

Linking all the men who were involved in the practical sciences were the instrument makers, skilled artisans who made precise mathematical instruments for surveyors, navigators, and astronomers. These tools (along with clocks) were the most sophisticated technological products of colonial America.

The first surveying and navigation tools used in the New World were brought from Europe. The expense and time involved in importing instruments encouraged the colonists to produce their own, and by 1800 a large number of the instruments being used in America were produced by native craftsmen. Some of these artisans in brass and wood emigrated from England and France where they had learned their craft. Other men learned to make instruments from published works on the subject or by copying European prototypes. Others served an apprenticeship under an established maker or attended school. There was also a substantial number of clockmakers who produced scientific instruments to meet the surveying and nautical needs of their communities.

The instrument maker played an important role in his community, and the nature of his work as a skilled and indispensable artisan insured his position as a member of the middle class. A characteristic that instrument makers shared with other colonial craftsmen was that they worked as individuals, shunning the guild system typical of Old World technology. They had pride in their special work, often announcing themselves on shop signs, on trade cards, and in newspaper advertisements as "makers of mathematical instruments."

Navigation Tools

Reflecting Octant

This tool was a precision instrument that made accurate determination of latitude possible. An 18th century invention, it was the result of a long and gradual evolution of tools to make marine observations. Its predecessors were the astrolabe, the cross staff, the back staff, and the quadrant.

Holding the octant vertically and looking through the eyepiece, the navigator sighted the horizon through the clear half of the glass on the opposite edge. Then, by moving the pointer along with the upper mirror, he was able to locate the heavenly object (the sun or a star) being used as a fix on the mirrored half of the glass. He then locked the pointer with a set screw and took his reading from the graduated arc. By consulting tables prepared by astronomers, an exact determination of latitude anywhere in the world could be made.

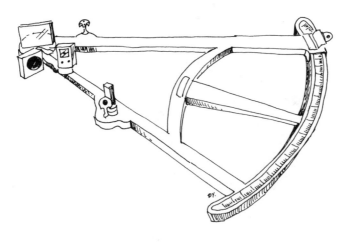

Marine Compass

Also known as the seaman's or mariner's compass, this was the simplest and most common of all the navigational instruments and took a minimum of skill to build. The marine compass consisted of three basic parts: the bowl or box (of wood or brass), the engraved compass card, and the magnetized needle turning freely on a pivot. It was used at sea for ascertaining and directing a ship's course by determining the vessel's position with respect to the magnetic meridian.

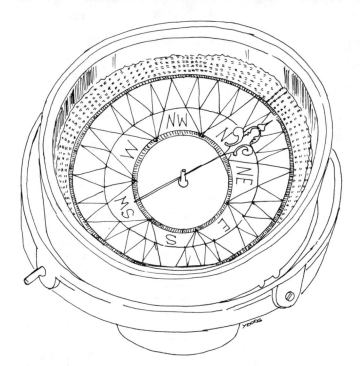

Surveying Tools

Surveying Compasses

The surveying compass, or circumferentor, was the instrument used by surveyors to measure angles until it was replaced by the theodolite in the 19th century. It was probably the instrument most needed and produced in early America. Many instrument makers produced compasses in both brass and wood in order to provide the trade with suitable tools in a flexible price range.

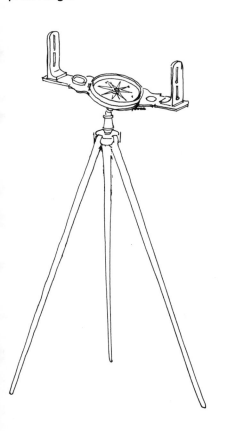

Wooden Surveying Compasses

The scarcity and expense of brass in early America led colonial instrument makers to seek substitutes. Because the basic element of the circumferentor is the magnetized needle, brass was the only hard metal that could be used. Wood, however, could be used in place of brass at only a fraction of the cost. It is probable that large numbers of wooden surveying compasses were made in 18th century America, though few have survived.

Brass Surveying Compasses

Although brass compasses were made in the 18th century, in general, the use of this metal for instruments did not become economically feasible until America began to produce brass in the early 19th century. Many superb examples of brass surveying compasses survive, some of them made by advanced scientific men ("mathematical practitioners") such as David Rittenhouse, Andrew Ellicott, and Owen Biddle.

Surveyor's Chain and Pegs

The surveyor's chain, or "Gunter's chain" (named after the English astronomer and mathematician who invented it in 1620) was used for taking linear measurements. Based on the English statute rod as a unit of measurement, the chain had 100 links and was exactly 66 feet, or 4 rods, in length. Using their chain and iron pegs, two men could measure straight lines and compute the area of a piece of land.

The wire link chain was gradually replaced by the modern steel tape, but some companies continued to advertise measuring chains until well into the 20th century.

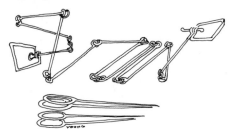

Tanning and Leather Working

History of Tanning

Tanning is the conversion of the skins of oxen, cows, and other animals into leather to prevent its destruction by putrefaction. The skins of animals were used as a covering by ancient man long before the tanning process was discovered, but they had to be kept dry as moisture would soon cause the skin to rot.

It is not possible to date the discovery of tanning, but reference to it is made in the Bible and it is known that the art had reached a high state of perfection by Roman times. Thought to have originated in the East, tanning was carried to Egypt and Greece and then to Europe. By the 11th century the principles of leather production were well established. However, operations were conducted with little regard for the chemistry involved, and it was not until the 19th century that this was defined and understood. Tanning was not initially affected to any major degree by the advent of the machine age. As late as 1840 it continued to be a craft that functioned chiefly as an adjunct to an agricultural society.

Tanning In America

The need for leather and the availability of hides from the fur trade and the slaughter of domestic animals facilitated the early establishment of tanneries in this country. Immense quantities of tree bark, source of tannin (the major chemical used in the tanning of leather), was easily obtained as the newly settled land was cleared. The first tannery was operating in New England in 1629, and in a few years tanning was an important industry throughout the colonies.

The making of leather was encouraged by colonial legislators, and at the end of the 17th century laws were passed establishing standards for the tanning of hides and regulating the location of tanneries to control the more unpleasant aspects of the trade.

The demand for food products in New York and Philadelphia stimulated the raising of cattle, which in turn yielded a large number of hides for local tanneries. New Jersey was a leading colony in the production of leather, and tanning was well established in Pennsylvania by 1653. By 1739 six tanyards were operating in Philadelphia.

With the quickening of trade in most areas of the country after 1700, raw hides were imported from the West Indies, Lisbon, and the Azores to supplement the domestic supply. Tanners in the vicinity of seaport towns traded finished leather for hides arriving by ship. The census of 1840 gave a rough estimate of 8,229 tanneries in the United States.

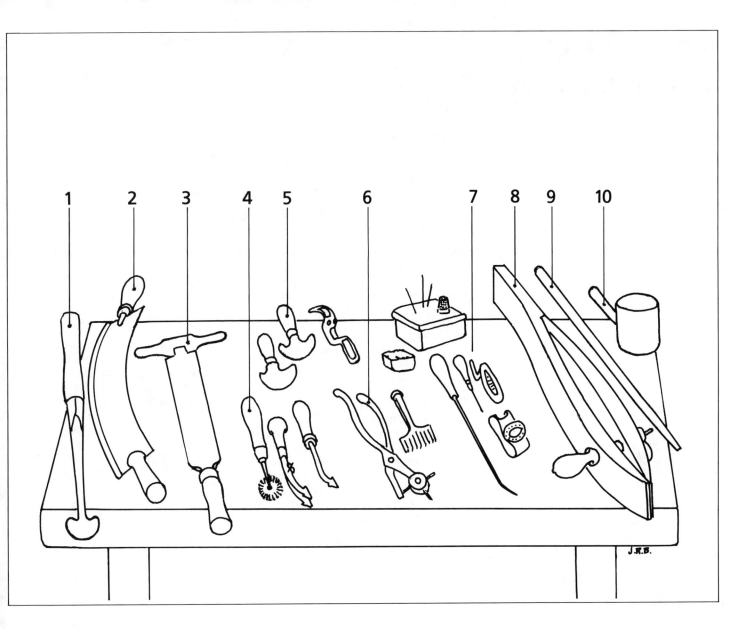

Tanning Tools

1. Bark Spud: After splitting the bark lengthwise with an axe, the bark spud was used to remove it in slabs. The slabs of bark were then dried and ground in the bark mill ready for use in making the tanning solution.

2. Unhairing Knife: Used on a concave beam to remove hair and excess flesh from the animal hide before the tanning process was started.

3. Head Knife: Used by the currier on a tanned animal skin stretched over a flat beam to reduce and equalize the thickness of the leather.

Harness and Saddle Making Tools

4. Marking Tools: Used by the leather worker to make a crease. The wheeled tool was used to mark stitching points in a line.

5. Cutting Tools: Used to cut and thin leather to shape and size before sewing together for harness parts or straps.

6. Punches: Used to punch holes and to make fancy and ornamental designs.

7. Sewing Tools: Used to make holes for sewing and to sew the edges and pieces of leather together in harness and saddle making. The large metal pieces are called palm irons and are used to protect the hand when pushing the needle through leather.

8. Clamp: Also known as a pair of clams. It was held between the knees to hold two pieces of leather together firmly while they were being sewn.

9. Stick: Used to force the straw into the body of horse collars to fill out and to pad them.

10. Mallet: Used to pound the stuffed bodies of horse collars to shape them and to make them firm.

Threshing & Winnowing

Ever since man began to grow grain crops (wheat, rye, barley, oats), he has had to thresh and winnow them after the harvest, so that the grain could be used for animal and human consumption.

Threshing

The process by which grain is separated from the stalk is known as threshing. Where adequate storage space was available, harvested crops were often stacked away in the barn to be threshed during the winter.

Before the introduction of machines for threshing, this job was performed by one of two methods: by driving draft animals over the unbound sheaves of grain spread out on the ground or barn floor; or by the use of a club-like tool called a flail. Both methods accomplished the same end—that of beating, and thereby dislodging the grain from the stalk.

The necessity for a proper threshing-floor was a determining factor in American barn architecture. An ordinary floor of loosely fitting planks would not do, because the grain would fall down into the cracks as it was being threshed. Threshing-floors were made of hard-packed dirt or of tightly-fitted boards, and were constructed inside the barn midway between two wide doors at either end of the building.

Winnowing

Winnowing is the process of separating threshed grain from the chaff (hulls of the grain seeds) and dust mixed with it after the threshing operation. The straw, from which all the grain had been beaten, was forked into a mow or loft to be stored and used for animal feed and bedding. The mixture of grain and chaff left on the floor had to be separated. This was accomplished by the ancient method of pouring or tossing it in a favorable wind. The wind blew the light chaff away, while the heavier grain fell back to the floor. In America, winnowing usually took place inside the barn, midway between two wide doors which provided a constant flow of air.

Machines known as fanning mills, or grain fans, were being used to winnow grain on some farms by the beginning of the 19th century. While more speedy and efficient than the old hand method of winnowing, fanning mills were unaffordable by many small farmers, and the old method continued to be widely used well into the 20th century.

After grain was thoroughly winnowed, it was stored away for animal feed, or shoveled into sacks to be taken to the mill for grinding into flour.

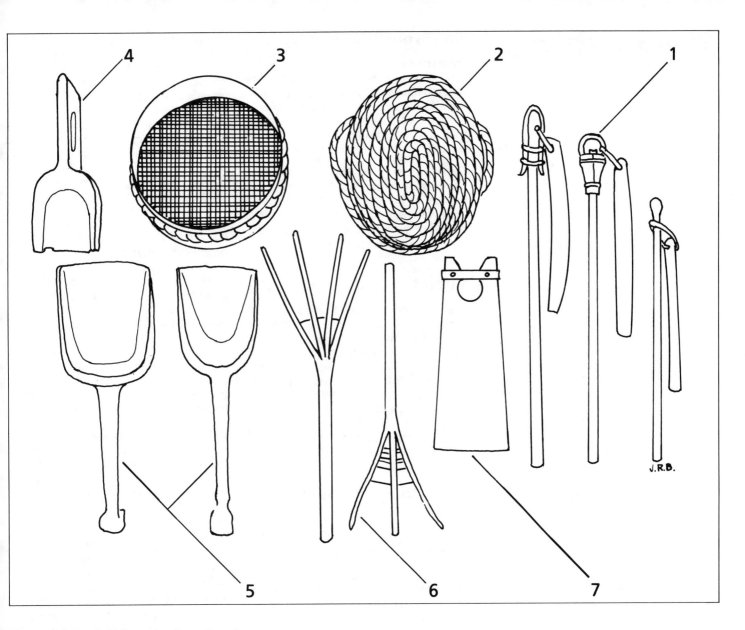

Threshing & Winnowing Tools

1. Flails: Universal tool for threshing. Consists of two rods connected with leather thongs. The long rod (hand-staff) was grasped with both hands and the short rod (swiple) was swung up and over the worker's head to be brought down with great force on the grain spread on the threshing floor. The force of the blow knocked the grain from the stalks.

2. Winnowing Basket: Shallow basket in which the grain and chaff mixture was placed for winnowing (separating). It was lifted up and the mixture was tossed into the air or poured out in a thin stream. The large two-handled wooden scoop on the floor was used for the same purpose, but required two workers.

3. Grain Riddle: Sieve used to remove coarse material, such as dirt and straw, from grain after it was threshed. Those displayed are made of wood, reed, horsehair, and vellum [animal skin].

4. Scoop: Used to shovel grain into sacks, barrels, or baskets.

5. Grain Shovels: Often cut from a single piece of wood with axe and adze. Used to move grain in the barn or granary.

6. Forks: Always made of wood, as were scoops and shovels. (It was believed that iron would bruise the grain.) Used to turn stalks of grain as they were being threshed, to assure that the bottom layers received the same treatment as the upper ones.

7. Corn Sheller: Used to remove corn kernels from the cob by scraping the cob against the sharp iron at the upper end.

Tinsmithing

Tin Throughout History

From the dawn of the Bronze Age about 5000 years ago, tin has played an important part in metallurgy. Tin possesses a remarkable ability to alloy with other metals, thus changing and improving their qualities. It is this property that has established its usefulness to society.

For many centuries, the main use of tin was in alloy with copper, to make bronze. By Roman times, it was being used with lead to make pewter. Most of the tin mined in Europe until the 16th century went into the production of pewter.

Tinplate

The revolutionary idea that thin sheets of iron could be plated with molten tin to produce "tinplate" occurred in Germany in the 16th century. "Tinning," as the process was known, was perfected in England. Tinplate, commonly known as tin, is the metal from which European and American tinsmiths made their amazing variety of wares. American tinsmiths imported their tinplate from England until the end of the 19th century.

Tinsmithing in America

Edward Pattison, a Scottish immigrant, settled in Berlin, Connecticut, in 1740, and began the commercial manufacture of tinware in America. Tin kitchen utensils were instantly popular, for they could be handled and cleaned with greater ease than the wood, pewter, and iron articles in use at the time.

The demand for Pattison's tinware grew rapidly, and by 1760 he had begun to teach other men his trade. Thus began an industry which would not only involve a large portion of the population of Hartford County, Connecticut for the next century, but would have a dramatic economic impact on all of New England. After a short suspension of business during the Revolution (all of America's tinplate was imported from England), the tin industry continued to expand, and by 1800 no American kitchen was complete without its supply of tinware. By 1810, so much tinware was being produced in Hartford County that it became necessary to seek a wider market. Master smiths, journeymen, and peddlers were sent to Canada, the South, and other settled areas to establish shops. By 1815, with foreign commerce and domestic industry stabilizing, smiths in Berlin, Connecticut alone (which remained the tinsmithing center of the country) were transforming 10,000 boxes of imported tinplate into tinware annually.

Throughout the first half of the 19th century, the number of shops involved in the production of tinware increased. By 1850, large tin-factories in the cities employed hundreds of workers and used several thousand tons of tinplate each year.

Master tinsmiths taught their sons and apprentices to make the same wares they made; in this way forms were handed down from one generation to the next. Working with tinplate, traditional hand tools, and hand-made patterns, the tinsmith made more articles used in the daily life of America than any other craftsman.

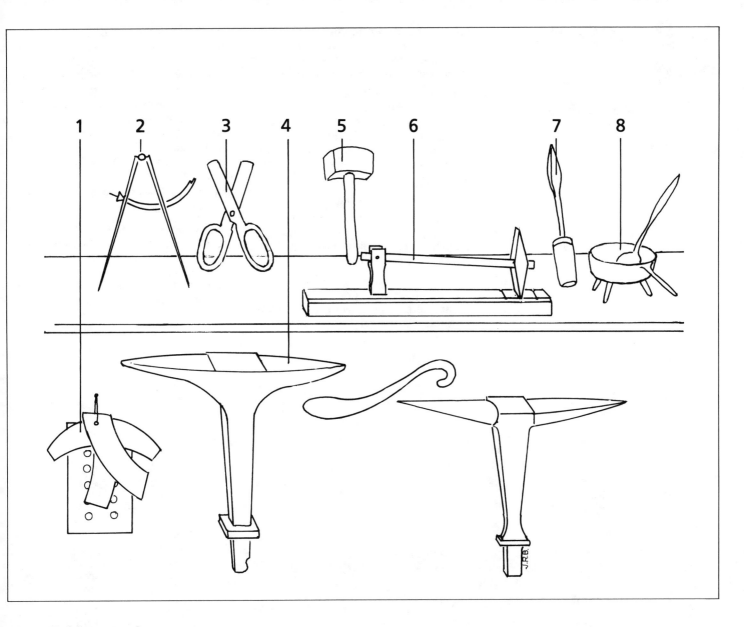

Tinsmithing Tools

1. Patterns: To form objects from flat sheets of tinplate, the tinsmith developed a pattern of the object as it would appear if laid out flat. He traced around the pattern (laid on the tinplate) with a sharp scribe, scratching a line to follow with his shears.

2. Wing Compass: A measuring and marking tool. The points could be opened to a certain measure and then placed on the metal and a mark made; or they could be opened to touch two points and then placed on a rule to find the measurement. Also used to scribe arcs and circles on metal.

3. Shears: Scissors-like tool for cutting sheet metal. They ranged in size from large bench shears to small hand snips.

4. Stakes: Specialized anvils of various shapes and sizes on which the tinsmith formed the cut out pieces of tin to the desired shape.

5. Mallet: Used to shape the tinplate over the stake.

6. Swedge: A hammer and anvil combined, with the hammer hinged to swing up and down on the anvil. Changeable parts gave a variety of combinations for making grooves and fluted edges on tinware.

7. Soldering Iron: A copper bit (head) set in an iron handle. Heated in a charcoal furnace, the head was held on a seam to melt solder into a joint, thus joining two pieces of metal.

8. Crucible & Ladle: Used to melt tin and lead together to make solder. The ladle was used to carry the molten metal to a bar-shaped mould, where it solidified into a shape and size convenient for use.

Toll Gates and Turnpikes

Toll Gates are wooden gates which were placed across privately owned roads and opened to allow traffic access to the road after payment of a fee.

Toll Gates were originally called "turnpikes," because in Medieval times they were actually poles or pikes that turned on a post to admit travelers. In time, roads with limited access for which a fee was charged came to be known as turnpikes.

Turnpikes in early America, as distinguished from the local roads of the same period, were highways, owned by private companies, upon which toll gates were erected.

Turnpikes were usually graded and surfaced with stone or gravel and were a great improvement over the often impassable natural earth roads common in America until the end of the 18th century. The first turnpike in Pennsylvania was the Philadelphia-Lancaster Pike. Between 1792 and 1828, one hundred and sixty-eight turnpike companies were formed and almost 3000 miles of road were built in Pennsylvania alone. In the latter half of the 19th century, control and management of turnpikes shifted from private corporations to local government.

Milestones were the original distance markers in this country.

Milestones are blocks of stone that were carved with the distance between cities and set in the ground alongside the road. They were later replaced by wooden and metal signs which showed direction as well as distance.

Turpentine Making

Turpentine, a colorless oil distilled from the sap of pine trees, has been an important product of American commerce since the 17th century.

Turpentine was used in the preparation of many products such as paints, varnishes, dyes, lamp fluids, and medicines. Important by-products of turpentine making were pitch, tar, and rosin. One of England's prime objectives in establishing colonies was to exploit the timber resources of the New World. Lumber to build her ships was needed, and great quantities of pitch, tar, and rosin were required to maintain and preserve them. Huge forests of pine were found growing in the southern colonies, and the manufacture and export of these products became a profitable business.

Turpentine sap was obtained by making V-shaped gashes in the tree trunk with the **Hack** or longer-handled **Puller**. The sap gradually flowed down the trunk into a cavity or "box" dug near the base of the tree with a **Box Axe**. The sap was then scooped out with a spade-like tool called a **Dipper**, into **Buckets**, ready for distilling in a nearby forest distillery. The **Scraper** was used to scrape dried sap off the tree face.

These tools were used in the "turpentine woods" of North Carolina in the mid-1800's.

1. Hack   4. Dipper
2. Puller   5. Bucket
3. Box Axe   6. Scraper

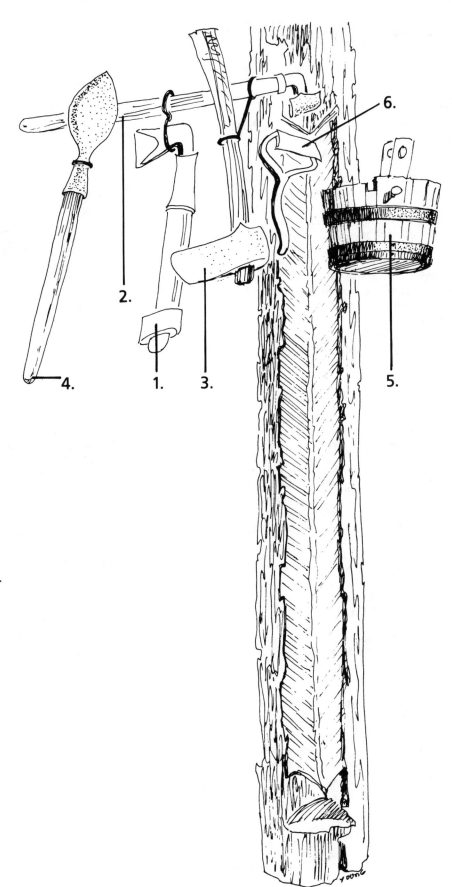

Transportation

Chaise

The chaise is a one-horse luxury vehicle that was used in America from about 1700 through the Civil War.

Known as a "shay", it had an adjustable hood and an ingenious suspension system, which accounted for its popularity. The body was suspended on leather straps called thoroughbraces, and the seat was mounted on wooden cantilevered springs, making it a relatively comfortable vehicle to ride in. The weight of the occupants was over the axle, thus it was well balanced and easy on the horse.

This type of chaise was known as the Boston or New England Chaise.

Spring Wagon

An important vehicle of the late horse-drawn era, the spring wagon was popular in both country and city.

The body was mounted on front and back elliptical springs and it had two to four removable seats. In rural areas, it served as a family and farm wagon. In towns and cities, it was used as a business wagon, with one or more seats removed. Variations of this type of wagon were made as late as 1920.

Light Wagon

Wholly American in origin, this type of one-horse wagon, also known as a pleasure wagon, first appeared in the early 19th century.

The seat was mounted on two wooden cantilevers and it had no springs.

Wagons and coaches made by the Abbott & Downing Company were renowned for their workmanship and durability.

Buggy

A buggy is any four-wheeled, one-horse carriage.

This type of buggy was known as a Coal Box Buggy because of its body's resemblance to a wooden coal box. It was introduced in 1862 and was popular for several decades. In order to avoid creases and to preserve the leather, the top was often allowed to fall half way back instead of being folded down tight. For this reason, it was also known as a Falling Top Buggy.

Buggies were handmade by highly skilled craftsmen: woodworkers, wheelwrights, blacksmiths, leather workers, and painters. Light in weight due to their hickory wood construction, buggies were durable and easy on horses. From 1830 until the advent of the automobile, the buggy was the most practical and popular two-passenger vehicle in America.

Sleighs

In the winter, in both rural and urban areas, horse-drawn sleighs took the place of wagons and carriages.

Snows were deep, roads were not plowed, and sleighs were the only practical way of getting about. Sleighs cost much less than carriages because of their less intricate construction, so almost every family had one. The ease and fun of traveling by sleigh made winter a favorite time for visiting friends. For over two centuries, sleighs of many styles and designs dominated America's winter roads. Early ones were built by wheelwrights with the help of blacksmiths. Later, they were produced by carriage builders. With the advent of automobiles and snow plows, sleighs became impractical and unnecessary.

Transportation

Stagecoach

In America before the coming of the railroad, one could go almost anywhere by stagecoach.

Between 1830 and 1850, most stagecoaches were built by the Abbott & Downing Company of Concord, New Hampshire, hence they were often called Concord coaches. In the East, light Concords rode the turnpikes. In the West, a heavier model became the standard passenger vehicle. This is a western stagecoach.

The Concord coach was springless. The body was suspended on leather thoroughbraces made of eight thicknesses or more of oxhide, supported by rigid iron stanchions. The coach was pulled by a matched team of six horses, although occasionally mules were used. The western Concords carried nine passengers inside and had seats for six more on top. Two guards usually rode beside the driver. Slowing and stopping was accomplished with the long-handled brake operated by the driver's right foot. On long downgrades, the wheels were sometimes chained.

After the coming of the railroad in 1850, stage transportation dwindled and stagecoaches finally disappeared from America's roads in 1910.

Conestoga Wagon

Conestoga wagons were distinguished by their great size and their distinctive "boat" shape.

The wagon and its team of six horses stretched up to sixty feet in length and could carry loads of up to six tons. The Conestoga was developed by the settlers of the Conestoga River Valley of Lancaster County, Pennsylvania, during the first half of the 18th century. Initially used for carrying farm produce and freight locally, this wagon was speedily adopted for freight hauling throughout the country and for all long overland migrations. The trails followed by these wagons became the main highways of eastern America.

Use of the Conestoga ended around 1845 when the railroads took over long distance freight hauling. Throughout the century, settlers continued to push westward in covered wagons called Prairie Schooners, the direct descendant of the Conestoga.

Fire Engine

Known as the Philadelphia Style Endstroke Pumper, this fire engine was the most powerful and efficient of its time.

Pulled to the fire by hand, it was operated by as many as 24 men, who worked the extended handles up and down. It drew water from a nearby cistern or hydrant and pumped it out at the rate of 200 gallons per minute for a distance of 180 feet.

In the first half of the colonial era fires were fought by people passing leather buckets of water hand to hand. The first hand-pumped fire engine in this country was imported to Boston from England in 1679. The first successful American-made hand-pumper was built in 1743. By 1850, steam-driven fire engines had begun to replace hand-pumpers. Philadelphia was foremost in the invention and manufacture of fire apparatus until the advent of the steam engine.

Bicycles

The Ordinary, ca. 1880: This High Wheeler, or Ordinary, as it later became known, had a front wheel four to five feet in diameter and a small rear wheel. It had solid rubber tires, wire spokes, and hand-operated brakes. The rider sat on a saddle high atop the big front wheel, with his weight placed fairly far forward. Serious accidents occurred frequently on these bikes. In spite of this, cycling grew in popularity, and by the end of the 1880's a new High Wheeler known as the Star had appeared.

The Star, ca. 1890: Named the Star by the New Jersey machine company which first manufactured it, this type of bicycle was considered safer than the Ordinary. The small wheel was placed in front of the big wheel instead of behind it.

In the 1890's, bicycles with equal sized wheels replaced the High Wheelers, and cycling became a national craze with lasting social and economic influences. Women were afforded the opportunity to participate in an active, outdoor sport, cycle clubs were formed everywhere, races were held constantly, and the first hard-topped roads were built. By 1900, hundreds of factories were producing millions of bicycles yearly.

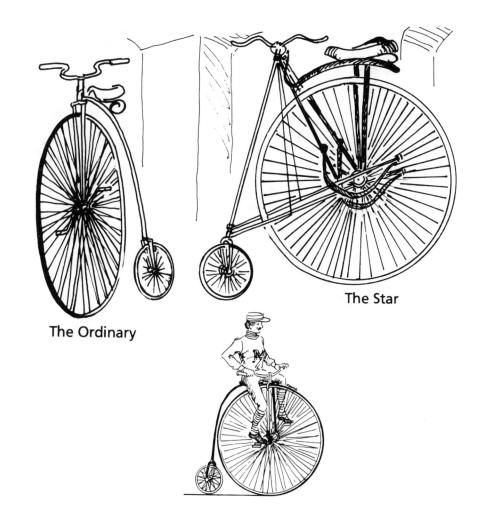

The Ordinary

The Star

Wallpaper & Fabric Printing

Wallpaper and Printed Fabrics in Europe

The first printed wallpapers and fabrics in Europe were imported from the Orient, where the technique of printing on paper and cloth had been used for centuries before it was known in Europe. By the end of the 16th century, the great demand for these imported luxuries and the newly-acquired knowledge of block-printing had resulted in the beginnings of the wallpaper and fabric printing industries in Europe. Because the methods of printing designs on cloth and paper are similar, the two trades have been closely related since their origins in the East.

"Painted papers," as the earliest wallpapers were called in France, were a cheap alternative to the tapestries and woven wall coverings which had been used for centuries to make rooms warm and liveable. The vogue for wallpaper spread rapidly throughout 17th century Europe, and wallpaper rose to occupy an important place in the decorative arts. Many engravers and artists of note became involved in its production. The art culminated in the great scenic panoramas of the 19th century that covered an entire room with a continuous landscape or pictorial narrative.

Printed fabrics from China and India were an article of commerce between the Orient and Europe long before the Europeans began to manufacture them. In 1696, calico printing (the word "calico" is derived from Calicut, an Indian seaport) was introduced into England. By the late 18th century, England led the world in the production, printing, and distribution of cheap cotton cloth.

Wallpaper in America

The earliest wallpapers in America were imported from England and France early in the 18th century. They were sold in "reams" or "quires" of small sheets which were pasted on the wall. They were sold by book-sellers, stationers, and upholsterers, and were also peddled from door to door.

By the end of the 18th century, there were manufacturers in Philadelphia, Boston, and New York, but America continued to look to Europe and to the Orient for the finest papers.

During the early years of the 19th century, a great demand arose, particularly in New England, for imported scenic wallpaper. The designs for these papers included historical subjects and events, panoramic views of well-known towns and cities, and subjects from mythology and literature. Their popularity is easily understood: they brought color, romance, adventure, and the lure of faraway places into homes which had formerly been largely without decoration.

In 1844, the first color printing machine was imported from England. As it had in Europe, the trade entered an era of mechanization and commercial development, and design and artistic merit became secondary to lower costs and increased production.

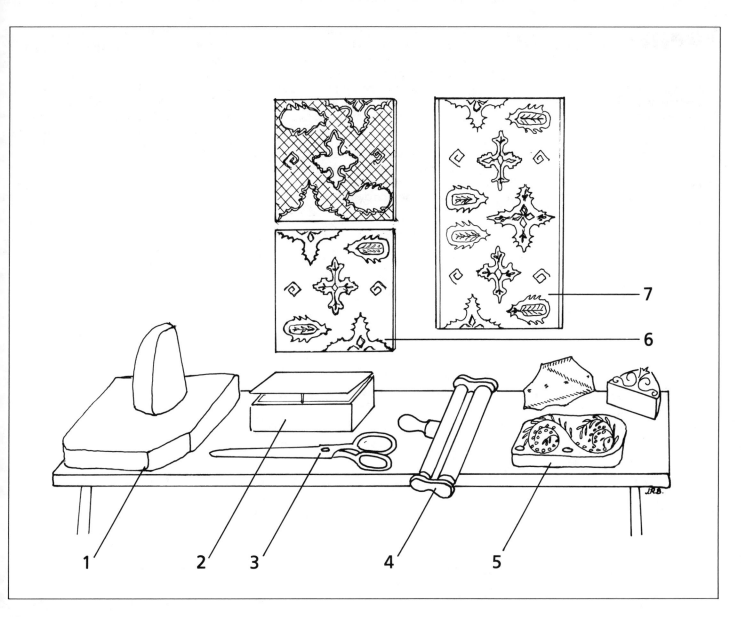

Wallpaper & Fabric Printing Tools

1. Paint Stone & Pestle: With the heavy stone pestle, dry pigments were ground to a fine powder on the slab. Mixed with the medium, they were then spread on the carved blocks for printing paper or fabric.

2. Pigment Box: For storage of color pigments.

3. Scissors: For trimming wallpaper strips so that the edges would match when pasted on the wall.

4. Rollers: Used to press the paper down onto the inked printing block that lay face up on a table, thus transferring the design from the block to the paper.

5. Fabric Printing Blocks: Hand-carved with knife, chisel, gouge, and mallet. The parts of the design that were too delicate to be cut in wood were laid in with metal lines and pegs. Some fabric printing blocks consisted solely of strips of copper set in narrow slots.

6. Wallpaper Blocks: Large wooden blocks were carved for every part of a wallpaper design. In the case of a repeating design, only a few blocks were needed. Some "scenic" papers required hundreds of carved blocks to print the various colors and parts of the design. One set of blocks could take several men a year or more to complete.

7. Wallpaper: Section of a strip of wallpaper printed from the adjacent blocks. The background was printed with the upper block; the design itself from the lower block.

Weathervanes

Mounted on the tops of buildings to indicate wind direction, weathervanes have been in use in America for over 300 years.

During the colonial period, designs were few and simple. Arrows, fish, roosters, Indians, and serpents prevailed. By 1800 there were dozens of subjects reflecting the localized interests of the American people. There were silhouettes of livestock on farm buildings, nautical motifs in seaport communities, and religious symbols on church steeples. American emblems such as Liberty, Uncle Sam, and Columbia adorned public buildings.

The earliest weathervanes were carved from wood or cut from sheet metal. By 1850, most weathervanes were being produced commercially. They were either cast in iron or molded from sheet copper over an iron pattern. The copper vanes, by far the most common, were hand finished with hammer and chisel, allowing the maker to follow his artistic inclinations. This provided variations even in weathervanes molded on the same template. Many weathervanes are considered to be among the finest examples of American folk art.

Sometimes a weathervane served as a storekeeper's or tradesman's shop sign, featuring a symbol appropriate to his business. This fancy three-dimensional wood and metal "plowman" served as a weathervane and a trade sign atop the Doylestown Agricultural Works for many years.

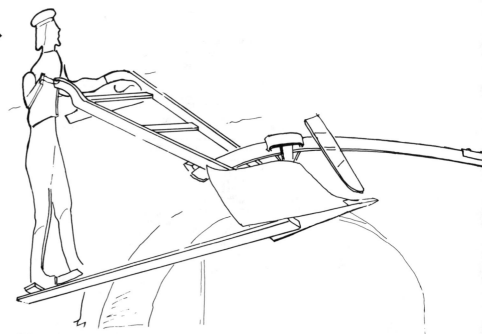

Well Sweep

The Well Sweep is an ancient apparatus used to ease the work of lifting water from a well.

It consists of four parts: the **post,** planted in the ground near the well; the **sweep pole,** thicker at one end than at the other to provide a counter weight;

the **bucket pole,** suspended from the end of the sweep pole; and the **bucket,** attached to the lower end of the bucket pole. The bucket was pulled down by a rope or chain fastened to the bucket pole. When the bucket was filled, the weight of the other end of the sweep pole raised it easily out of the well.

Well Sweeps were widely used in America prior to the invention of pumps and survived in some areas until the 20th century. Because the upright post that was planted in the ground rotted away after about 15 years, most well sweeps have been lost.

YOUNG

Whaling

Whaleboat

This 30 by 6 foot boat from New Bedford, Massachusetts carried six men and all the gear necessary to catch and kill a whale.

The whaleboat was renowned for its light weight, ease of handling, large carrying capacity, and its seaworthiness.

Whaling ships carried four to six of these boats, ready to be launched when a whale was sighted. Long ropes lay coiled in tubs, and harpoons and lances were kept ground and sharpened. The harpoon, attached to one end of the rope, was used to capture the whale. When a whale was harpooned, it often sounded (dove), taking out the entire length of rope. Sometimes a harpooned whale would tow the boat at great speeds until it tired. This was popularly known as a "Nantucket Sleighride." When the whale tired, the boat drew near and the chief officer (known as the boatheader or

lancer) killed the whale by piercing its lung with the lance. The whale was then towed back to the whaler and the removal, cutting up, and rendering of the blubber into whale oil began. Whale oil was used as fuel in lamps and as a machine lubricant.

Whaling was an unpredictable, often dangerous business. Some ventures were highly profitable and made fortunes for Yankee "whalemen." Other whaling trips resulted in great financial loss due to disaster and misfortune at sea.

Whaling Tools

These hand-forged iron tools were used on board whaling ships to render whale blubber into whale oil.

Whale oil was used to light America's homes, towns, and lighthouses until the late 19th century and was used as a machine lubricant until very recently.

After a whale had been killed, it was tied to the side of the mother ship and the process of stripping the blubber from the whale, using the **Cutting Spades,** began. The blubber, cut into heavy strips, was hoisted aboard using the **Blubber Hook** suspended from a pulley and windlass.

Pikes and **Forks** were used for moving and tossing pieces of blubber around the deck. The **Mincing Knife** was used to cut the blubber into thin strips, ready to be rendered or "tried out"—boiled in huge iron pots called **Try-Pots.** The **Skimmer** was used to remove bits of scrap from the boiling oil. After cooking for about an hour, oil from the blubber was removed from the pot with **Ladles** and stored below deck in wooden barrels. A single whaling ship might bring home as many as 2000 barrels of oil.

These whaling tools came from New Bedford, Massachusetts, which was a whaling center because of its deep water ports and railroad connections.

1. Cutting Spades
2. Blubber Pike
3. Mincing Knife
4. Blubber Fork
5. Bailer
6. Skimmer
7. Blubber Hook
8. Try-Pot

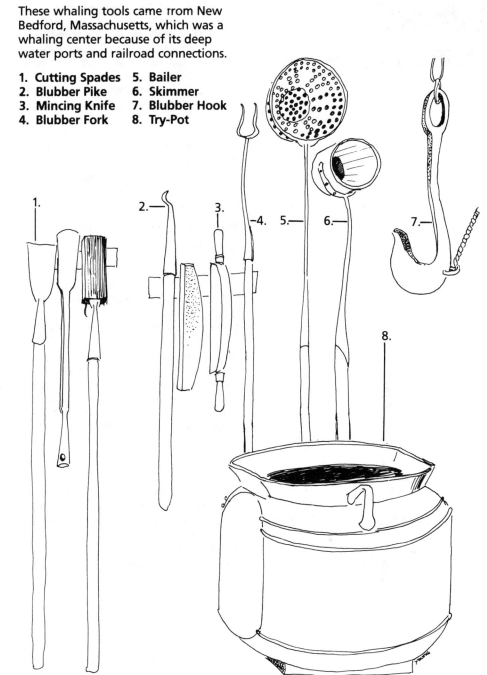

Wheel-wrighting

The Wheel in Antiquity

The wheel ranks among the foremost of man's technological discoveries. It is generally believed that it was invented around 3500 B.C. in Mesopotamia. The first wheels were made of three wooden planks cut to form a circle and clamped together with two wooden struts. By 2000 B.C., spoked wheels were being made in the Near East, Egypt, Greece, China, and Europe. By 500 B.C., Celtic wheelwrights were building wheels and wagons whose quality was not surpassed for many centuries.

The Wagon in Europe and America

For many centuries, wagons were used mainly for baggage and transport. Known as carrier wagons in England, they were drawn by teams of up to twelve horses and could carry eight tons of weight. The ancient two-wheeled ox cart was the standard farm vehicle until about 1700. At that time, a demand arose for a wagon suited for farm use, and village wheelwrights began to build small wagons of three or four tons capacity which could be drawn by two horses.

Sophisticated wagon-building skills were brought to America by the English and German settlers of eastern Pennsylvania. Their greatest achievement was the Conestoga Wagon. First used for hauling farm produce and freight in the early 1700's, the Conestoga was speedily adopted for overland migrations and

haulage of freight throughout the country. Around 1845, the railroads took over most of the freight traffic, and wagon-builders turned to building smaller, simpler wagons.

The Wheelwright

The wheelwright was a maker of wheels and most often a skilled carpenter as well, making entire wagons and carts. Many wheelwrights also made agricultural tools and sleighs.

Wheelwrighting was one of the most important of all trades, and the 19th century wheelwright's shop was a vital part of America's past. Shops prospered throughout the country. They were run by a master wheelwright, perhaps a journeyman, and invariably a young apprentice. Most often, the ironwork on a vehicle was sent out to the local blacksmith; some wheelwrights did their own "ironing" or blacksmithing work.

By the last quarter of the 19th century, machines had largely replaced hand tools in the production of wagons. Many wheelwrights became assemblers of factory-made hubs, spokes, and rims, working in their own shops or in a factory.

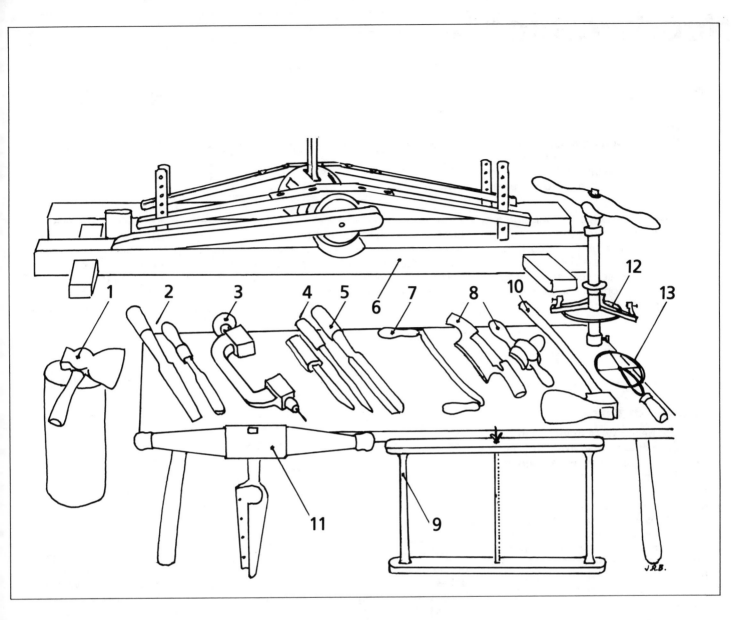

Wheelwrighting Tools

1. Axe: Used to cleave oak for spokes. Made with a right- or left-handed offset, with the blade ground on the opposite side.

2. Gouges: Used to form elm logs to the shape of a hub in the lathe.

3. Brace & Bit: Used to drill hole in the hub to start the mortice into which the foot of the spoke was driven.

4. Chisels: Various sizes; used to remove excess wood from the mortice.

5. Buzz or Bruzz: A V-shaped chisel for squaring the corners of mortices.

6. Wheel-Frame: Adjustable wooden frame which held a wheel upright during repair or while pounding spokes into the hub. The parallel sides could be adjusted to hold hubs of various sizes.

7. Drawknife: Narrow, flat, straight blades of various sizes used for trimming spokes.

8. Spokeshave and Jarvis: Shaves used for rounding and smoothing spokes.

9. Bettye Saw: Frame saw, used with an up and down motion, for cutting the felloes (curved sections of rims).

10. Adze: Used for hollowing the insides of felloes. It is similar to that used by house carpenters except that the blade is more curved.

11. Hub Reamer: A large taper auger used for forming the hole through the hub for the axle.

12. Hub Boring Machine: Alternative to the hub reamer, this machine bored out the hub to take the iron axle box. When the bar was turned, the cutters revolved, removing a shaving of wood as they moved through the hub.

13. Traveler: Metal or wooden wheel used for measuring. It was rollled around the rim of the wheel and the number of turns were counted. It was then rotated the same number of turns along an iron strip, giving the exact length needed to make a tire for that particular wheel.

Woodworking

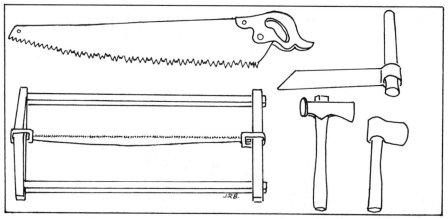

Roughing

While the saw mill was one of the earliest industrial enterprises in most communities, the woodworkers of early America necessarily prepared much of their lumber from rough sawn planks or from log "butts" which had been cut to convenient lengths.

The **crosscut saw** was used for rough cuts across the grain. Crosscutting requires the removal of quite a bit of sawdust, so crosscut blades have widely spaced teeth or special short teeth placed every so often which serve only to carry the sawdust out of the cut.

Frame saws with centrally mounted blades were used for "ripping" planks along the length of the grain into smaller boards. Some frame saws had the blade mounted on one side of the frame (the "bow" saw). These could be fitted with ripping or crosscutting blades. Log butts could be split into boards called clapboards with a **froe**. The froe was positioned on the log and the back of its blade was struck with a mallet. **Hatchets** were used for all kinds of trimming and splitting.

Rough Surfacing

Logs and beams were shaped with the adze or with the broad axe. The hoe-shaped head of the **adze** was slightly rounded, making this an ideal tool for hollowing or for smoothing concave surfaces. Carpenter's adzes were swung with both hands towards the feet. Smaller, one-handed adzes were also used. The **broad axe** was a short-handled, large-bladed tool designed to square logs. Its head was slightly offset to allow clearance for the user's hands as the tool was swung past the work.

Drawknives of many shapes and sizes were used for removing rough spots,

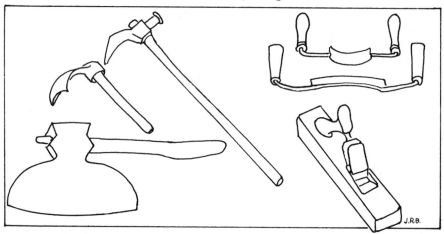

trimming clapboards, carving wheel spokes, shaping barrel staves, making shingles, and carving other cylindrical shapes like chair legs.

The **jack plane** looks like other bench planes, but it had a slightly concave blade so that it could rapidly remove any unevenness left by the saw, adze, axe, or drawknife without tearing the wood. The jack plane prepared the wood for final smoothing.

Fine Surfacing

Smooth, flat surfaces were formed with a selection of specialized **bench planes**. The longest one, the **jointer plane** (24"-36"), was used for smoothing edges on boards. The shortest, the **smoothing plane,** was used to touch up rough spots in a finished piece.

Mouldings and curves in straight boards were made with **moulding planes**. There are hundreds of moulding planes, each with its own uniquely shaped blade. Some, like the sash plane, the ogee plane,

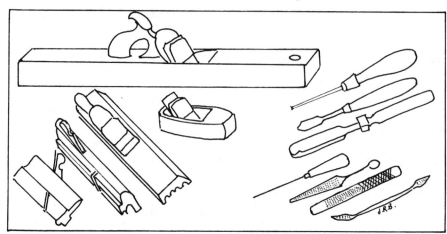

or the crown moulding plane, cut quite specific shapes. Round and hollow planes of various sizes could be used in combinations to make almost any shape. A joiner's tool box might contain as many as 30 moulding planes.

Irregular hollows and shapes were formed with **gouges** which came in a variety of standard shapes and sizes. **Files, rifflers,** and **rasps** were valuable supplements to gouges before sandpaper came into general use.

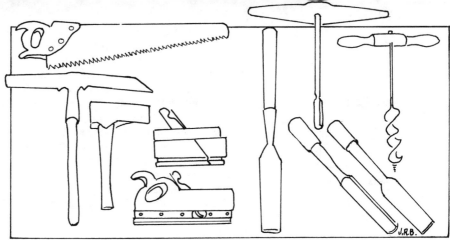

Rough Fitting

The basic joint for all framing timbers was the mortise and tenon. The tenon was easily cut with a **hand saw,** but the mortise required specialized tools. Short-handled **mortising axes** or T-shaped **twibils** could be expertly swung to form a rough mortise. The large **firming chisel** was used to square holes that had been drilled by **augers.** Early augers had spoon-shaped bits. The development of the **spiral auger** at the beginning of the 19th century eased the process of cutting mortises con-

siderably. A more exact mortise could be produced with a **mortising chisel.** Chisels were struck with hardwood mallets.

The basic joint for edge-joining boards was the tongue and groove. A pair of

tongue and groove planes was used to make this joint. One plane cut the tongue, and a matched plane cut the groove. Occasionally both of these functions were built into one dual purpose plane.

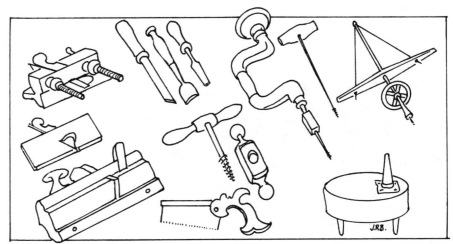

Fine Fitting

The many joints common to cabinet work were made using various combinations of **chisels** and specialized planes. Chisels were used to cut mortises, to remove material between saw-cut notches or dovetails, and for precise trimming. Special planes were used to cut grooves so that boards could be fitted together. The adjustable **plow plane** cut a groove parallel to the edge of a board, the **rabbet plane** cut a groove in the edge of a board, and the **banding plane** cut wide valleys in boards.

Tenons and dovetailed joints were cut with fine-toothed **tenon saws** that were often fitted with a rigid spine. Holes for all purposes were drilled with **braces and bits, bow drills,** and several types of T-handled **augers.** Joints were often pinned

with dowels that might be made with a **peg cutter** mounted on a stand. Wooden screw threads in drilled holes were cut with **taps. Screw boxes** were used to thread dowels that had been turned on a lathe.

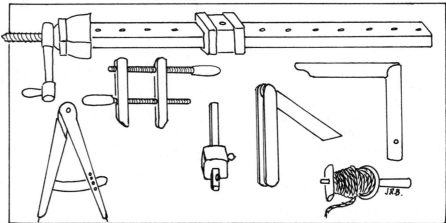

Holding and Measuring

The woodworker's most valuable holding tool was his bench. Vises, hold downs, and stops on the bench allowed him to secure his work firmly in almost any position. Long **cabinet maker's clamps** and smaller **hand screw clamps** were used for gluing and for other special holding jobs.

Compasses were used for marking circles, constructing figures, and dividing circles. The **marking gauge** had an adjustable

face that could be set at a chosen distance from a fixed blade or joint. Sliding the gauge along the edge of the work scribed a well defined line. Mortises were commonly laid out with a marking gauge. Angles were laid out and marked

(with a pencil or a scribe) with either a **square** or an adjustable **bevel.** The bevel was particularly useful for accurately marking dovetails. The **chalkline** and **plumb bob** were simple but indispensable tools for framing buildings.

Lathes

Great Wheel Lathe

A lathe is a machine which holds a piece of wood or metal between two centers and turns it so the work can be shaped by hand-held "turning chisels" similar to carpenters' chisels.

This lathe, known as a Great Wheel Lathe because of the huge wheel used to power it, was used by two generations of Bucks County woodworkers until about 1895. It was capable of turning much larger and harder pieces of wood than earlier foot-operated lathes, which were used to shape such things as chair and spinning wheel parts. The large flywheel, turned by an apprentice or helper, was connected to the spindle of the lathe by a leather strap. It spun the lathe with great speed, enabling woodworkers and wheelwrights to turn heavy work such as wheel hubs, mill shafts, and large bed posts.

The lathe has been in use in many countries of the world for about 3000 years. This type, powered by a wheel and strap, first appeared in the 15th century. The smaller lathe exhibited also has a flywheel, but it was powered by means of a foot treadle rather than a hand crank.

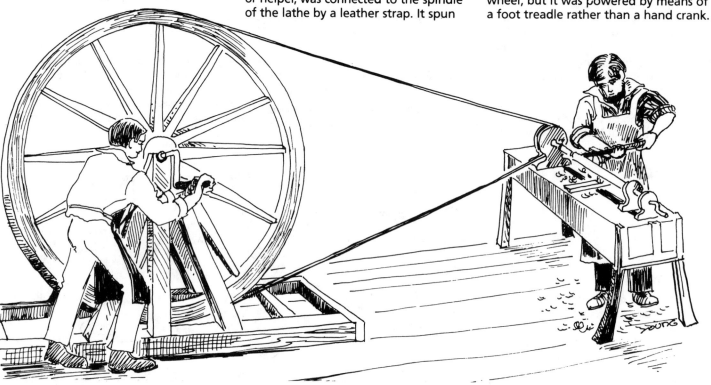

Pole Lathe

Also known as a Spring-Pole-and-Treadle Lathe, the Pole Lathe was driven by a cord fastened to the end of a springy wooden pole secured above the lathe.

The cord was wrapped around the work being turned, and the other end was attached to a treadle hinged to the floor. When the turner stepped on the treadle, the work rotated rapidly in one direction. When he lifted his foot, the elasticity of the pole pulled the cord back, causing the work to rotate in the opposite direction. This is known as "alternating motion," as opposed to continuous motion of the work in one direction, which was achieved with the introduction of the Great Wheel Lathe in the 15th century.

The Pole Lathe probably first appeared in Western Europe in the 2nd half of the 12th century. It was a great improvement over earlier lathes, which were powered by a bow, and was quickly adopted by turning shops all over Europe. Wood was turned on Pole Lathes in America until well into the 19th century, and in some parts of the world they are still used.

Wooden Water Pipes and Pumps

Wooden pipes and pumps were used on farms and in cities of 19th century America to transport water from springs and reservoirs or to pump it from wells.

Lead and iron pipes had been in use for centuries, but the expense of casting and transporting metal pipe made it impractical. Wooden pipe, on the other hand, was economical and readily made just about anywhere in America.

A wooden pipe was made by boring a hole through the center of a log with a long-handled **Auger** of small diameter. The hole was then enlarged with **Spoon Bits** and **Reamers,** which often came in graduated sets. A sawhorse-like stand was used to support these heavy iron tools while in use. Pipes—usually ten to fifteen feet long—were tapered at one end and reamed out at the other so they could be fit together. Pitch or tallow was often used to seal the joints.

Wooden pumps consisted of a piston-like bucket with a leather flap in its bottom moving up and down a section of vertical pipe. When the pump bucket (connected to the pump handle) went down, the flap opened, letting water into the upper part of the pipe. When the bucket came up, the flap closed, trapping the water. It took several pumps of the handle to trap enough water above the bucket to come out the spout.

Index

Index